Writing to Learn
THE SENTENCE

Teacher Edition

Writing to Learn
THE SENTENCE

Teacher Edition

LOU J. SPAVENTA
MARILYNN L. SPAVENTA
Santa Barbara City College

Boston   Burr Ridge, IL   Dubuque, IA   Madison, WI   New York   San Francisco   St. Louis
Bangkok   Bogotá   Caracas   Lisbon   London   Madrid
Mexico City   Milan   New Delhi   Seoul   Singapore   Sydney   Taipei   Toronto

McGraw-Hill Higher Education

*A Division of The **McGraw-Hill** Companies*

WRITING TO LEARN: THE SENTENCE, TEACHER EDITION

Published by McGraw-Hill, an imprint of the McGraw-Hill Companies, Inc., 1221 Avenue of the Americas, New York, NY 10020. Copyright © 2000 by The McGraw-Hill Companies, Inc. All rights reserved. No part of this publication may be reproduced or distributed in any form or by any means, or stored in a database or retrieval system, without the prior written consent of The McGraw-Hill Companies, Inc., including, but not limited to, in any network or other electronic storage or transmission, or broadcast for distance learning.

This book is printed on recycled, acid-free paper containing 10% postconsumer waste.

2 3 4 5 6 7 8 9 0 QSR QSR 0 9 8 7 6 5 4 3 2 1

ISBN 0-07-232732-4

Vice president and editor-in-chief: *Thalia Dorwick*
Editorial director: *Tina B. Carver*
Developmental editor: *Aurora Martinez Ramos*
Marketing manager: *Pam Tiberia*
Senior project manager: *Peggy J. Selle*
Production supervisor: *Sandy Ludovissy*
Senior designer: *Amy Feldman*
Supplement coordinator: *Sandra M. Schnee*
Compositor: *David Corona Design*
Typeface: *11/13 Stone Sans*
Printer: *Quebecor Printing Book Group/Dubuque, IA*

Cover/text designer: *Juan Vargas*
Cover illustration: © *PhotoDisc Inc., 1999*

Library of Congress Cataloging-in-Publication Data

Spaventa, Louis J.
   Writing to learn / Louis J. Spaventa, Marilynn L. Spaventa. — 1st ed.
    p. cm.
   Includes indexes.
   Contents: [bk. 1] The sentence — bk. 2. The paragraph — bk. 3. From paragraph to essay — bk. 4. The essay.
ISBN 0-07-230753-6 (bk.1) — ISBN 0-07-230754-4 (bk. 2) — ISBN 0-07-230755-2 (bk. 3) — ISBN 0-07-230756-0 (bk. 4)
   1. English language—Textbooks for foreign speakers. 2. English language—Rhetoric—Problems, exercises, etc. 3. Report writing—Problems, exercises, etc. I. Spaventa, Marilynn. II. Title.

PE1128.S697   2000
808'.042—dc21   99-057820
                                                                          CIP

www.mhhe.com

CONTENTS

Preface xi
    To the Instructor xi
    Acknowledgments xiv
    To the Student xv
    Notes to the Instructor xvii

Unit One: Myself and Others

Chapter 1

A. Prewriting 2
    Exercise 1. Telling stories 2
    Exercise 2. Writing sentences 3
    Exercise 3. Introduce yourself 4
    Exercise 4. Alphabet line up 4

B. Structure 4
    Exercise 1. Manuel's story: Identifying subjects and verbs 4
    Exercise 2. Tran's story and Yoshi's story: Writing verbs 5
    Exercise 3. Identifying ourselves: Verb forms 6

C. Writing and Editing 6
    Exercise 1. Why do you study English? 6
    Exercise 2. Your story 7
    Exercise 3. Editing practice 9
    Exercise 4. More editing practice 10

D. Journal Assignment 11

Chapter 2

A. Prewriting 12
    Exercise 1. Telling stories 12
    Exercise 2. Retell the story 13
    Exercise 3. How do you learn English? 13
    Exercise 4. How do your friends learn English? 13
    Exercise 5. A poem about learning English 14
    Exercise 6. What I can do 14

B. Structure 15
    Exercise 1. Identifying singular and plural subjects 15
    Exercise 2. Who studies? 16
    Exercise 3. Writing verbs that end in *-y* 17
    Exercise 4. Interview with a classmate 17

C. Writing and Editing 18
  Exercise 1. Writing new sentences 18
  Exercise 2. Writing sentences about yourself 19
  Exercise 3. Rewriting sentences using *and* 19
  Exercise 4. Compare your sentences 19

D. Journal Assignment 19

Unit Two: Family and Relationships
Chapter 3
A. Prewriting 20
  Exercise 1. Matching 20
  Exercise 2. My life 21
  Exercise 3. Talking to a classmate 21
  Exercise 4. Writing about your family 22

B. Structure 22
  Exercise 1. The verb *be*—present and past 22
  Exercise 2. Writing sentences with *be* 23
  Exercise 3. Using *be, get, go, have, do* 24
  Exercise 4. Rewriting sentences 25
  Exercise 5. Group dictation 25

C. Writing and Editing 26
  Exercise 1. Editing for usage 26
  Exercise 2. Word order 26
  Exercise 3. Sentence order 27
  Exercise 4. Write your story 27
  Exercise 5. We are the same. We are different. 28

D. Journal Assignment 29

Chapter 4
A. Prewriting 30
  Exercise 1. Discover the story 30
  Exercise 2. Carol is. Carol isn't. 32
  Exercise 3. What were you? 33
  Exercise 4. What are you? 33

B. Structure 34
  Exercise 1. *Years ago* and *now* 34
  Exercise 2. Complete the sentence 35
  Exercise 3. Interview a classmate 35
  Exercise 4. Writing *he* or *she* 36

C. Writing and Editing 37
  Exercise 1. Editing for past tense and negative 37

Exercise 2. Editing for present tense, past tense, and negative   37
Exercise 3. Reviewing time order   38

D. Journal Assignment   38

Unit Three: Education
Chapter 5
A. Prewriting   40
Exercise 1. Match the sentence with the picture   40
Exercise 2. Vocabulary hunt   42
Exercise 3. Word dictation   42
Exercise 4. Tell a story   42

B. Structure   43
Exercise 1. Regular verbs in past tense   43
Exercise 2. Present tense to past tense   43
Exercise 3. Learning irregular past tense verbs   44
Exercise 4. Past tense and present tense   45
Exercise 5. Practice with negation   45

C. Writing and Editing   46
Exercise 1. Capitalization and punctuation practice   46
Exercise 2. Reading notes   47
Exercise 3. Recalling a story   48
Exercise 4. Writing sentences about school   49
Exercise 5. What was good about it?   49

D. Journal Assignment   49

Chapter 6
A. Prewriting   50
Exercise 1. Who am I?   50
Exercise 2. Am I like Oskar?   51
Exercise 3. Comparing yourself   52
Exercise 4. I like. I don't like.   52

B. Structure   53
Exercise 1. Verb + verb: **Like to, want to**   53
Exercise 2. Verb + verb: **Like + -ing**   53
Exercise 3. Verb + verb: I don't like studying, but I have to study.   54
Exercise 4. Verb + verb: Using the correct form   55

C. Writing and Editing   56
Exercise 1. Oskar in elementary school   56
Exercise 2. Oskar in high school   56
Exercise 3. Oskar in English class   57
Exercise 4. Give advice to Oskar   58

D. Journal Assignment   59

Unit Four: Work

Chapter 7

A. Prewriting 60
Exercise 1. Read, practice, and match   60
Exercise 2. Create a story   61
Exercise 3. Exchanging stories   62
Exercise 4. Filling out a questionnaire   63

B. Structure 63
Exercise 1. Information questions   63
Exercise 2. Facts about you   64
Exercise 3. Where do you come from? How do you get there?   64
Exercise 4. Class travel chart   65

C. Writing and Editing 65
Exercise 1. Abdullah's conversations   65
Exercise 2. Abdullah's bad day   67
Exercise 3. A bad day at work   67
Exercise 4. Reading and asking questions   68

D. Journal Assignment 69

Chapter 8

A. Prewriting 70
Exercise 1. Finding the story   70
Exercise 2. Creating characters   72
Exercise 3. Defining tools   72
Exercise 4. The day   73

B. Structure 74
Exercise 1. Revisiting the story   74
Exercise 2. Using pronouns   74
Exercise 3. A conversation   75
Exercise 4. A poem to remember   76

C. Writing and Editing 77
Exercise 1. Editing for pronouns   77
Exercise 2. Editing for time order   77
Exercise 3. Questions about work   78
Exercise 4. Writing about your work   79

D. Journal Assignment 79

Unit Five: Leisure and Recreation

Chapter 9

A. Prewriting 80
Exercise 1. Vocabulary building   80
Exercise 2. Talking about hobbies   81

Exercise 3. Sports and exercise 82
Exercise 4. Describing a picture 82

B. Structure 83
Exercise 1. Forming the continuous tense 83
Exercise 2. What's happening? 84
Exercise 3. Pronouns and adjectives 85
Exercise 4. Relaxing 86
Exercise 5. Using *not* with the continuous tense 86

C. Writing and Editing 88
Exercise 1. Describing a scene 88
Exercise 2. Editing the story 88
Exercise 3. Imagining yourself a star 89
Exercise 4. Editing for details 89

D. Journal Assignment 89

Chapter 10
A. Prewriting 90
Exercise 1. Matching sentences with pictures 91
Exercise 2. Free time activities 91
Exercise 3. The television guide 92
Exercise 4. At the movies 92

B. Structure 93
Exercise 1. Using the demonstrative adjectives, *this* and *that* 93
Exercise 2. Demonstrative adjectives, *these* and *those* 94
Exercise 3. *This, that, these* and *those.* What have you got? 95
Exercise 4. Another look at the pictures 95

C. Writing and Editing 96
Exercise 1. Editing the story 96
Exercise 2. Putting the story in order 96
Exercise 3. Imagine yourself 97
Exercise 4. Giving feedback on your partner's story 98

D. Journal Assignment 99

Unit Six: The Natural World
Chapter 11
A. Prewriting 100
Exercise 1. Labeling the pictures 100
Exercise 2. Making categories 101
Exercise 3. What happened? 101
Exercise 4. Changes in your hometown 102

B. Structure 103
Exercise 1. What has happened? 103
Exercise 2. Another look at the pictures 104

Exercise 3. Things we still do   104
Exercise 4. Your classmates' experience   105

C. Writing and Editing   106
Exercise 1. Edit the conversation   106
Exercise 2. My favorite place   106
Exercise 3. Writing a story   108
Exercise 4. Reviewing capitalization and punctuation   108
Exercise 5. Nature's friend   109

D. Journal Assignment   109

Chapter 12
A. Prewriting   110
Exercise 1. Where would you rather be?   110
Exercise 2. What's there?   111
Exercise 3. More vocabulary   111
Exercise 4. Wild places   112

B. Structure   112
Exercise 1. Where would you rather go?   112
Exercise 2. I've never, but I'd like to   113
Exercise 3. What can you do there?   113
Exercise 4. Making choices   114

C. Writing and Editing   114
Exercise 1. Editing for tense   114
Exercise 2. Continuing the story   115
Exercise 3. Writing about a wild place   115
Exercise 4. Group editing project   115

D. Journal Assignment   115

Appendix I: Basic Capitalization and Punctuation Rules   117
Appendix II: Spelling Rules for Verbs   118
Appendix III: Verbs   120
Appendix IV: Journal Writing   123
Glossary of Grammatical Terms   124

PREFACE

To the Instructor

WRITING TO LEARN is a four-book ESL writing series aimed at adult learners of English from diverse educational backgrounds. The series focuses both on the process of writing and on writing as a product. The goal of the series is to help students learn how to write for academic and vocational success. Each book in the series makes use of student skills and experience to generate writing topics while providing guided practice of appropriate vocabulary and grammar, English writing conventions, writing, editing, rewriting, and journal writing. Each chapter of the first three books in the series begins with a visual image that leads to discussion and writing. The fourth text uses readings as prewriting prompts. WRITING TO LEARN begins with an elementary text designed to improve student ability to write accurate and descriptive English sentences. The upper elementary to intermediate level text focuses on writing paragraphs. The third or intermediate level text takes the student from paragraph writing to organizing, writing, and editing essays. The final book at the advanced level concentrates on improving student essay writing skills and enhancing essay writing style.

Each book in the series is divided into six units. Books 1 and 2, *The Sentence* and *The Paragraph,* have two chapters in each unit while books 3 and 4, *From Paragraph to Essay* and *Writing Essays,* have just six units each. The reason for the difference is to create more and shorter lessons for the elementary to lower intermediate levels, and fewer but longer lessons at the intermediate to advanced levels of writing.

Here are the unit themes:

Unit One: Myself and Others

Unit Two: Family and Relationships

Unit Three: Education

Unit Four: Work

Unit Five: Leisure and Recreation

Unit Six: The Natural World

Students who work through several texts in the series will have the opportunity to explore the same theme from different perspectives.

The use of icons to indicate pair and group work is meant to facilitate classroom organization while eliminating repetitive instructions. Notice that the number indicates the total number of students needed to form the group. Be sure to follow each chapter in the Instructor's Edition for helpful suggestions and instructions for activities that are not included in the student text.

Organization

Each unit and chapter is divided into the following four sections:

A. Prewriting In *The Sentence,* each chapter begins with prewriting activities based on a picture story. Prewriting activities include vocabulary learning, pair work, group work, and discussion. It is important to begin writing lessons with something to talk about the words necessary to talk. We encourage a lot of conversation before the student writes.

B. Structure Grammar activities include review of the basic English grammar necessary for the writing in the chapter. While the structure section introduces grammar with example, explanation, and practice exercises, *The Sentence* is not meant to be a grammar text. Grammar has been incorporated as a tool for expressing one's thoughts rather than as an end in itself.

C. Writing and Editing Activities in this section are devoted to improving writing skills, especially employing the vocabulary and grammar practiced in sections A and B. Activities in this section develop from controlled to creative practice. You will notice that we have not included sample student sentences and paragraphs for students to follow in the writing section. In many texts, writing samples are provided with the expectation that students will diligently work with the sample to produce their own personalized writing. In fact, this rarely happens and students are more likely to be constricted by the model. In this series, the writing models appear in the structure and editing sections to encourage students to alter the samples and make the language their own.

D. Journal Assignment The personal, unedited, daily writing practice that journal writing affords is an important part of the process of writing well in English. To introduce students to journal writing, there is a journal writing assignment at the end of each chapter in this first book. Other texts in the series provide more extensive lists of topics. These assignments allow students to synthesize and expand upon what they are studying in each unit.

You will need to decide how you will respond to student journal writing. Here are a few suggestions.

- Respond only to the content of what is written in the journal.
- Look for positive examples of vocabulary and grammar usage consistent with each chapter and highlight or underline them in student journals.
- Tell students you are going to read their journals with an eye toward a particular kind of writing: a descriptive sentence, an opinion, a comparison, an analysis or explanation, and so on. Then identify that writing when you come across it in student journals.

- Ask students to read something from their journals during class time. Ask the students listening to respond in writing to what they hear.
- Each week, read selected journal entries aloud to the entire class to inspire and foster respect among students of each other as writers.

Appendices   Each text contains appendices of grammar and writing conventions for student reference. During your first class meeting, when you familiarize students with the book, make sure you take some time to point out the appendices and what they contain. Students too often discover appendices at the end of a course.

Instructor's Edition   The Instructor's Edition of *The Sentence* contains chapter-by-chapter notes of explanation, advice, suggestions, and reproducible quizzes for each chapter.

Web Site   The *Writing to Learn* web site can be located through the McGraw-Hill, Inc. web site at <www.mhhe.com>. This interactive site should be useful to instructors and students. For instructors, the site can be a virtual teacher's room where instructors can raise questions and exchange ideas and activities related to this series. Students can post and read writing assignments for each chapter and thus expand the walls of their classroom.

The Sentence

This first book in the series emphasizes writing on the sentence level. However, because picture stories are used to elicit vocabulary, discussion, and student opinion, the instructor will also find it easy to order the sentences into a paragraph based on the picture sequence in each chapter if he or she chooses to do so. Some exercises in the book give students the opportunity to see what paragraphs look like because the exercise involves manipulation of language within a paragraph. However, students are not required to write unguided paragraphs to succeed in using the text. So one goal of the text is to focus on student production of good sentences, and another goal is to expose students to the form of the English paragraph.

The First Lesson

Begin your first class with an exercise that helps your students become familiar with this text. You can do this orally, in writing, or both. Students might work in pairs or small groups. A familiarization exercise is contained in the **To the Student** part of the introduction to *The Sentence*.

Question your students about the names of the six units, the number of chapters in each unit, the number of sections in each chapter, the number and names of the appendices, and their thoughts about the use of each chapter section and appendix. Create and distribute a follow-up activity that reviews the text organization.

If you do the exercise orally, use the cooperative question-and-answer technique called "Numbered heads together." Have each student in a pair or group count off—1, 2 or 1, 2, 3, 4. Tell the class that before you call on anyone to answer, students who know the answer in a pair or group should tell the answer to their partner or group mates. Then pick a number. When you call "Number 1" for example, only students who are "Number 1" may raise their hands to answer. If the answer is correct, go on to the next question. If it is not, ask another "Number 1." In this way, you can begin teaching students to rely on their partners or group mates. We encourage students to turn to each other as resources for language learning. This is an essential element of process editing.

Acknowledgments

First and foremost, we acknowledge the debt of thanks we owe to our students at Santa Barbara City College, whose interests and concerns were the catalyst that led us to embark upon this writing project. We would like to thank as well our colleagues at City College and in the larger field of ESOL writing, who often made valuable suggestions to us about our manuscripts.

This book and this series would not have been written without the encouragement and persistence of Tim Stookesberry, Aurora Martínez, and Pam Tiberia at McGraw-Hill, and of our series editor, the inimitable, indefatigable, and empathetic Bob Hemmer.

Should you have any suggestions or comments, we would be happy to receive them from you in writing, via email, or at our web site. You can write to us care of the ESL Department, Santa Barbara City College, Santa Barbara, California, 93109, USA. Our email address is spaventa@sbcc.net.

Lou and Marilynn Spaventa
Santa Barbara, California

To the Student

Welcome to *The Sentence!*

The goal of this book is to help you write good English sentences. The book has six units. Each unit has a topic. You will discuss the topic. You will write about the topic. The topic for Unit One is Myself and Others. Look for the topics of the other units. Look in the Table of Contents. Write the names of the topics below.

Unit One   _Myself and Others_____

Unit Two   _____

Unit Three   _____

Unit Four   _____

Unit Five   _____

Unit Six   _____

Now look at Unit One. How many chapters are there?

If you said "two," you are right. Each unit has two chapters. How many chapters are there in the book? Your answer _____

Take five minutes to skim (look quickly) through the chapters. Look only at the first page of each chapter. Then close the book. Write down whatever words come into your mind. Write down words about what you saw.

_____

_____

_____

Each chapter has four sections. Match the section with its description. Draw a line from the section to its description.

Section	Description
Prewriting	gives ideas for writing on your own in a journal
Structure	practices English grammar
Writing and Editing	prepares you for writing by learning vocabulary and giving ideas to discuss
Journal Assignment	has exercises to improve your writing skills

Preface

Your instructor will decide how to use this book in the best way for you. Please write in this book. Write words and sentences. We designed *The Sentence* as a workbook. The book is for reading and writing. So please write in it.

Now you have met our book, *The Sentence.* Your instructor may ask you some questions about the book. Be prepared to answer them. We hope you enjoy working with the book. Remember that learning to write well is a skill. You need to practice a skill to get good. Write a lot. Write what you feel and what you think. Learn a lot!

Lou and Marilynn Spaventa

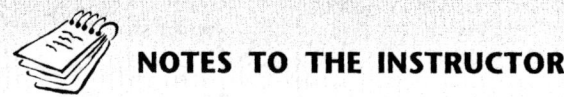

NOTES TO THE INSTRUCTOR

TO THE INSTRUCTOR

Writing to Learn: The Sentence

Unit One

Chapter 1

Part A. Exercise 3 Your students may need some help with the directions for this exercise. You can easily guide the students by motioning to them to stand in two lines and by modeling how they are to ask questions and respond. One purpose of this exercise is to get students talking by asking and answering questions even though students probably have not studied question formation yet. Students will be asking the same question several times, which will give them the opportunity to develop confidence and fluency. Another purpose of this exercise (and Exercise 4) is to get the students out of their seats and provide the opportunity for everyone in the class to participate at the same time.

If most of your students come from the same country, the responses to these questions will be the same or similar. In that case, to make the exercise more interesting, you can ask students to choose a country and their answers will correspond to the country that they chose. If students are creative, the result can be amusing.

Part A. Exercise 4 The purpose of this exercise is for students to practice orally the same skill that they will use in peer editing. It is not an easy skill! It requires students to work collectively on a task, check their work, and make appropriate corrections. Students must work together, work independently from the teacher, demonstrate knowledge of alphabetical order *and* listen to each other. They must also be able to identify their first name and their last name. After students line up alphabetically, it is important to have everyone check and correct as the names are called out.

Part C. Exercise 1 This type of exercise reappears in later chapters. It is important that students have the opportunity to express their ideas and opinions. Be sure that they understand that they are to check only the reasons that apply to them. Students should be encouraged to add other reasons but may need your help with vocabulary.

Part C. Exercise 2 Drawing pictures is an excellent way to organize information, and students often find that it is easier to speak if they have visual support. Some students may feel inhibited by a lack of artistic ability. A good way to reassure these students is to draw your story about learning another language on the board with simple stick figures and write simple sentences as a model.

Part C. Exercise 4 This exercise builds on what students have learned in Exercise 3. Here students are also required to recognize where the second sentence begins. Doing the first one or two items together on the board will help students. You may also wish to have students underline the subjects and verbs to help them recognize where the second sentence begins. Let the students know that this is a more challenging exercise and reassure students who make mistakes.

Part D For many students, this is their first introduction to journals. Most will need help understanding the purpose of a journal and what is expected of them. Take a few minutes to

- discuss the purpose of journal writing
- explain that journal writing benefits students at all levels
- explain that journal writing is a requirement of many classes in the United States
- explain your expectations regarding, for example, fluency vs. accuracy, how often and how much students should write, clarify when you will collect journals and how you will respond to the writing
- model on the board how you would complete this first assignment

Some instructors prefer to designate a particular kind of notebook for journals such as college blue books or composition books. Sometimes students more readily understand that journal writing is a distinct kind of writing when they have a distinctive book to write in. Refer to Appendix IV on page 123 for information to the students about journal writing.

Chapter 2

Part A. Exercise 5 Memorizing poetry is beneficial on many levels. You may want your students to memorize the poem and perform it in class either in pairs or small groups. Volunteers can be invited to recite for the class.

Also be sure to point out to students that standard rules of capitalization and punctuation do not apply to poetry.

Part A. Exercise 6 This exercise first asks students to list words from the poem that they know well. Second, they are asked to write any sentences that they like and any words that they can pronounce well. Their sentences do not need to relate to the poem. It should be interesting to see what students choose to write. Be sure to give them the opportunity to share their sentences and pronounce their words.

Part B. Exercise 2 Students may not know the meaning of all of the words to identify the places where people study. Ask for volunteers to give sample sentences that demonstrate the meaning of the words. Write the sample sentences on the board. You can supply sentences for words that no student knows.

Part B. Exercise 4 This exercise and others in future chapters permit students to converse with controlled grammar and vocabulary. It is important that students read the questions aloud to their partner rather than doing this as an individualized reading comprehension exercise. One variation is to have one partner read the question silently, close the book, look directly at his or her partner, and then ask the question. The question and answer roles should be reversed. Another variation, similar to Exercise A.3 in Chapter 1, is to line up students face to face and call out a word. Students will then use this word to form a question. Use this variation only after students have had pair practice.

Part C. Exercise 2 As in previous exercises, it is important that students write only those sentences that are true for them.

Writing to Learn: *The Sentence*

Unit Two

Chapter 3

Part A. Exercise 1 This exercise involves new vocabulary such as *aunt, nieces, nephews, grandparents,* and *church.* Students probably have not yet studied the irregular past forms of verbs either. Encourage students to make guesses based upon what they *do* know. Taking risks, tolerance of ambiguity, and making educated guesses are important for language learners. Be sure to make your students comfortable by reassuring them that what individuals do not know, pairs or the entire class may know.

Part A. Exercise 3 Anticipate that students will make mistakes forming grammatically correct sentences. You may choose to ignore the mistakes to encourage experimentation and communication, or you may choose to write the questions on the board for students to use as a model.

Part A. Exercise 4 You may wish to encourage students to experiment and write true and interesting sentences that are not necessarily related to the picture story by writing a few of your own sentences on the board. *My mother is a beautiful woman. My father has a moustache.* Encourage students to help each other with vocabulary and be ready to circulate among the students to help with language they need to express their ideas.

Part B. Exercise 2 This is a good exercise to have different students write sentences on the board. The class can then check to see if the sentences are comprehensible and if the correct verb form is used. In this way, you can easily check the students' work and provide reinforcement of the new verb forms for the entire class.

Part B. Exercise 3 You can anticipate several common errors in this exercise. This exercise is somewhat difficult because students must be concerned with usage *and* form.

- Many Spanish speakers will supply *have* for sentence 1.
- Students may use *go* for sentence 3. Making that mistake will give you an opportunity to point out the necessity of using *to* with *go,* which is illustrated in sentence 4. Sentence 7 introduces one of the exceptions: *go home.*
- Using *get* (sentences 6 and 8) is probably the most difficult for students who try to translate.
- There are two correct answers for sentence 9: *are* or *have.*

Students will have the opportunity to practice using these verbs in the following two exercises.

As a follow-up activity, give the students a short self-quiz at the beginning of the next class. Write the following sentences on the board and have them test themselves so that they can feel a sense of confidence.

1. I _____ homework in my kitchen.

2. My friend _____ a letter every Saturday.

3. He _____ thirty years old.

4. She _____ to the supermarket every Friday.

5. They _____ home after class.

Notes to the Instructor

Unit Two

Chapter 4

Part A. Exercise 1   Students should be able to "learn" the new vocabulary by looking at the pictures and eliminating the sentences that do not belong. Encourage guessing to build confidence rather than using a dictionary.

Part B. Exercise 1   The completed charts may reveal a lot about students' pasts and will thus provide the opportunity for students to get to know each other better. Be sure to allow time for students to share their charts in small groups and encourage follow-up questions and conversation.

Part B. Exercise 3   Students may not have studied question formation yet and will certainly not have mastered it. However, it would be artificial to ignore the need to ask and answer questions. Therefore, you will need to give students a lot of assistance in forming their questions. You may wish to work on the board first, pointing out the two basic patterns they will need: *Were you _____?* and *Did you + base form of the verb _____?*

Unit Three

Chapter 5

Part C. Exercise 2   Be sure that students understand that they are to use the notes to tell the story in complete sentences. You can model by telling the first sentence or two or asking for a student volunteer to tell the first sentence or two.

Unit Three

Chapter 6

Part A. Exercise 4   To set up this exercise, start with yourself. Have the class ask in chorus, "What do you like?" Answer with noun phrases. Answer one thing each time the class asks the question. The class keeps asking until you run out of things to mention. Now choose a student to sit in front of the class. The rest of the class asks the question in chorus. Then, as the instructor, you take the lead in answering about things you don't like. Again, continue until you run out of ideas. Then, get another student to volunteer. You can break students into groups of five or six and have them continue the exercise, or you can have the student who has just answered choose someone to take his or her place.

Part B. Exercise 3   Be sure to explain that the list of *verb + verb* combinations is only a partial list. Students should also understand that there is no rule to apply here. They need to memorize the *verb plus gerund* or *verb plus infinitive* combinations and this can best be done by practice. You may need to give example sentences to be sure that the students understand the meaning of all of the verbs.

Unit Four

Chapter 7

Part A. Exercise 1   Model one or two of the dialogues first so that the students can concentrate on intonation.

Part A. Exercise 1, item #5   Some teachers only teach the object form *whom* for formal speech. These dialogues are informal and most native speakers would not use *whom*. You can explain this to your students and guide them to use the form that you think is most appropriate.

Part B. Exercise 4   Direct the class to give you their written answers from Exercise 3. Make a large chart on the board or on an overhead transparency. As you do this, direct the students to make the same chart in their notebooks.

Name	Place	Transportation	Time

Now record the students' information on the chart or have the students record it. When the chart is complete, ask students to write sentences like the following:

Lou comes from New York.

He came here by plane. (note past tense)

It takes five hours.

Have students write information about five or six of their classmates.

Part C. Exercise 3   Some students may not have work experience. If so, encourage them to be imaginative and invent a story.
   There are several ways to bring this exercise to closure.

1. If you want to emphasize vocabulary, you can start a chart on the board and encourage students to come to the board and write useful or new vocabulary as they hear it in the stories. After the exercise is finished, you can have a volunteer create a sentence with each word.

2. You can have students compare writing by having each group select the best (most complete or most creative) from each group to read to the entire class. If the class is large, you can save time and maintain a higher level of student interaction by having the selected writers rotate to new groups to share their writing. This rotation can continue for several rounds.

Notes to the Instructor

Unit Four

Chapter 8

Part A. Exercise 1 Many details have been included in the picture to allow for vocabulary expansion. The pictures also lend themselves to abstract vocabulary such as "responsibility" and words of emotions.

> **Picture 1:** wheelchair, uniform, give birth, have a baby, take blood pressure, patient, nurse, bouquets of flowers, balloons

> **Picture 2:** changing table, crib, bumpers, mobile, dresser, tired, exhausted, stressed out

> **Picture 3:** desk, photograph, manager, computer, responsibility, stress

> **Picture 4:** briefcase, calculator, cell phone, suit, tie, bottle, feed, comfort, laptop computer, check email

Part A. Exercise 2 Reassure the students that there are no correct answers; they should use their imagination. They may need help with language to express a problem for each job. To simplify the exercise, you can have students rate job satisfaction as *high, medium,* or *low,* or *good, ok,* or *bad.*

Part A. Exercise 4 Before the students complete the schedule, point out that the husband or wife may do an activity for more than one hour. For example, you can write on the board 8:00, 9:00, 10:00, 11:00, 12:00 in brackets and "works in his office in the hospital."

Before the oral part of this exercise, you may want to call attention to the use of *at* and **from X:00 to X:00** to anticipate the language needed for accuracy.

You may wish to review basic parts of speech (subject, verb) as introduced on page 5.

Part B. Exercise 3 This dialogue introduces the idiomatic usage of *I bet* and *funny.* Be sure to check to see if the students understand these expressions and can provide synonyms.

Part B. Exercise 4 This poem provides you with possibilities: you can emphasize rhythm and pronunciation. (Carolyn Graham's books are excellent resources for ideas on how to do this.) You can have students read chorally, in groups, or you can have students take turns in groups reading from memory.

Part C. Exercise 3 Students may need help understanding all of the questions. Rather than encouraging translation, you can circulate around the room while students are working to give examples of answers or to reword questions.

Unit Five

Chapter 9

Part A. Exercise 1 Remind students, as they do this exercise, to add *too* at the end of the statement. They have practiced this before (page 28).

Practice of the present continuous tense appears in the Structure section (Part B) of this chapter. It is likely that students have already practiced or been exposed to this tense, but you may wish to model the responses on the board so that the students can follow a pattern as they complete the exercise.

Part A. Exercise 2 Review the list of hobbies together as a class before students circulate to ask questions. They will need help determining which verbs to use: *play chess, collect stamps, garden,* and so on. Students will need similar assistance for the following exercise (3).

Unit Five

Chapter 10

Part A. Exercise 2 You may wish to put a time limit on the activity and have a prize for the group with the most answers. Students may need to use dictionaries.

Part C. Exercise 3 You may wish to have students make a simple drawing before writing the story.

Unit Six

Chapter 11

Part A. Exercise 4 By giving a few of your own examples on the board, you may encourage students to come up with at least five differences. Point out that changes can be positive or negative.

Part B. Exercise 1 Most grammar texts do not introduce the present perfect tense at the beginning level. However, students will hear this tense and will need it to express their ideas in writing. The intention here is to give students an introduction to this tense, which they will practice more at the intermediate level.

Part C. Exercise 2 Stress to students that it is not important to have artistic talent. The intent is to use drawing as a prewriting activity. You may want to model your own drawing on the board. Before students begin the question phase, they can ask you the questions.

Part C. Exercise 5 Be sure that students understand that they should add more than one word to complete each line. After students have read their poems aloud in groups, you may have them choose one to read aloud to the class, or you may choose to have them post the poems around the room.

Unit Six

Chapter 12

Part A. Exercise 2 Students may need help coming up with the vocabulary for this exercise. You can encourage them to use dictionaries, ask each other, or ask you by describing or miming.

Divide the board into four parts as in Part A. Exercise 2. Have a student from each group write his or her group list on the board. This chart can be used again after students decide where to place the vocabulary in Exercise 3.

Part A. Exercise 3 This vocabulary may be somewhat difficult for some students. Students should be able to guess which picture *dry, windy* and *rainy* go with but will have more difficulty with others. If there are no guesses for particular words, try miming or give examples they may know.

Part B. Exercise 1 Have students (without books or pens) move to the biggest empty space or spaces in the classroom. Ask them to choose a side and talk to a partner after they hear the choices. For example, you will ask, "Would you rather go to a jungle (pointing to one side of the room) or a desert (pointing to the other side of the room)?"

Students will move to their choice and then find a partner to explain why. Students may change sides and partners for each choice. If students do not understand the vocabulary, miming or examples will help to clarify.

Part C. Exercise 4 In this text, peer editing exercises have emphasized content and clarity rather than spelling and grammatical accuracy. In this exercise, students are asked to edit on the sentence level. Some students are very sensitive about having other students correct their mistakes, and some students make inaccurate corrections. These problems should be lessened because students are working as groups.

Your Name _____   Quiz: Unit 1, Chapter 1

Instructor's Name _____   Date _____

Part A. Subject and Verb Underline the <u>subject</u> one time and the <u>verb</u> two times.

   EXAMPLE: My <u>teacher</u> <u>speaks</u> English.

1. I study English.

2. My friend lives in Toronto.

3. Students do homework every night.

4. She works at night.

5. My classmates come from different countries.

Part B. Verb Forms Write the correct verb forms. Some verbs need **-s**.

   EXAMPLE: He ____speaks____ two languages. (speak)

1. I _____ English as a Second Language. (study)

2. My friend _____ homework. (love)

3. He _____ help. (need)

4. They _____ computers. (like)

5. She _____ from Australia. (come)

Part C. Capitalization and Punctuation Write these sentences with correct capitalization and punctuation.

   EXAMPLE: she loves to learn
   She loves to learn.

1. andi speaks russian and english

_____

(Continued)

2. does your teacher speak chinese

   _____

3. mariana comes from brazil and speaks portuguese

   _____

4. he and i study together

   _____

5. where does she live now

   _____

Your Name _____   **Quiz: Unit 1, Chapter 2**

Instructor's Name _____   **Date** _____

Part A. Subject and Verb   Underline the <u>subject</u> one time and the <u>verb</u> two times.

>   **EXAMPLE:** Her <u>teacher</u> <u><u>studies</u></u> Chinese.

> Dat comes from Vietnam. He speaks Vietnamese and a little English. His grandfather lives in Vietnam. His father lives in Canada.
>
> My cousins live in Texas. They study English and work. They love Texas. I want to visit them.

Part B. Verb Forms   Write the correct verb forms. Some verbs need **-s**.

>   **EXAMPLE:** He ____*speaks*____ two languages. (speak)

> There are many interesting people in my class. Mariko _____ (come) from Japan. She _____ (speak) Japanese. She _____ (want) to learn English and Spanish. Josefine and Mario _____ (come) from Mexico. They _____ (work) in the same restaurant. They _____ (study) together, too. Mary _____ (come) from Macedonia. She _____ (like) to talk to everyone. Eduardo _____ (come) from Chile, and he speaks Spanish. I _____ (like) this class!

(Continued)

Part C. Spelling   Write the correct form of the italicized verbs.

   EXAMPLE: I *study* English. She ____studies____ Spanish.

1. I never *cry* at sad movies. He always _____ at sad movies.

2. I *say*, "Yes." He _____, "No."

3. I *try* hard. She _____ hard, too.

4. I never *worry* about tests. He always _____ about tests.

Part D. Editing for Capitalization and Punctuation   Correct the following sentences.

   EXAMPLE: where does your sister live she lives in new york
   Where does your sister live? She lives in New York.

1. where does your teacher come from she comes from florida
   _____

2. there are many places to visit i want to visit every state in the united states
   _____
   _____

3. my grandfather lives in my country he wants to come here
   _____

4. what language does he speak he speaks russian
   _____

Quiz: Unit 1, Chapter 2 (Concluded)

Your Name _____   Quiz: Unit 2, Chapter 3

Instructor's Name _____   Date _____

Part A. The Verb *Be* Write the correct present tense form of the verb **be**.

    EXAMPLE: My daughter ____is____ 5 years old.

1. I _____ from another country.

2. Where _____ you from?

3. They _____ in the computer lab.

4. He _____ a student.

5. You _____ never late.

Part B. The Past Tense of the Verb *Be* Write the correct past tense form of the verb **be**.

    EXAMPLE: I ____was____ a good dancer.

1. He _____ a teacher in his country.

2. They _____ late yesterday.

3. I _____ a good child.

4. We _____ here last week.

5. She _____ absent yesterday.

Part C. The Present Tense and Past Tense of the Verb *Be* Write the correct present or past tense form of the verb **be**.

    EXAMPLE: I ____am____ not hungry now, but I ____was____ very hungry before lunch.

1. He _____ a good soccer player in high school, and he _____ a good soccer player now.

2. They _____ residents of this country now, but they _____ not residents of this country last year.

(Continued)

3. You _____ early today, and you _____ early yesterday, too.

4. She _____ an intelligent little girl, and she _____ an intelligent woman.

Part D. Verbs: *Get, Go, Have, Do, Be* Write the correct present tense form of the verbs in parentheses.

    EXAMPLE: He ____*goes*____ home after class.

1. I _____ a big family.

2. She _____ homework every night at 8:00.

3. You _____ twenty-one years old.

4. We _____ have a small family.

5. I _____ to the computer lab every day.

6. They _____ from France.

7. He _____ his paycheck on Fridays.

Your Name _____   Quiz: Unit 2, Chapter 4

Instructor's Name _____   Date _____

Part A. Editing for Verb Form, Present Tense Circle the correct form of the verb.

EXAMPLE: I (am, is) a student.

> Edmundo (come, comes) from Mexico. He (is, are) married, and he (have, has) three children. His children (go, goes) to elementary school. They (get, gets) a lot of homework every night. They (do, does) the homework every night at the kitchen table. Edmundo (need, needs) to learn English. He (want, wants) to help his children study.

Part B. Editing for Verb Form, Past Tense Circle the correct form of the verb.

EXAMPLE: I (am, was) a student last year.

> Ming (is, was) a student in his country last year. He (does not want, did not want) to study in his country. Now he (is, was) a student in my class.
>
> Stefan (isn't, wasn't) in class yesterday. Now he (isn't, wasn't) here again.

(Continued)

Part C. Negative Write the negative form of sentences in the chart that are not true.

EXAMPLE:

Not True	True
My grandfather is an elementary school student.	My grandfather isn't an elementary school student.

Not True	True
1. The President of the United States is an ESL teacher.	
2. Today is Sunday.	
3. My teacher was an ESL student last year.	
4. The teacher was absent every day last week.	
5. I do homework in the bathtub.	

Part D. Time Order Write the sentences in the correct order.

I got married in my country, and I had children. We came to the United States in 1990. In my country not many students study at university. Now we all study and speak English. I was a good student in elementary school. In high school, I was a good student, too.

_____

_____

_____

_____

Quiz: Unit 2, Chapter 4 (Concluded)

Your Name _____   **Quiz: Unit 3, Chapter 5**

Instructor's Name _____   Date _____

Part A. Regular Past Tense Use the words to make a sentence in the past tense. Be sure to use correct capitalization and punctuation.

    EXAMPLE: the teacher / work / hard
    The teacher worked hard.

1. my kindergarten teacher / smile / all the time

_____

2. the children in my class / practice / reading and writing the alphabet

_____

3. everyone / walk / to school

_____

4. we all / like / lunch and play time

_____

5. I / play / with everyone

_____

Part B. Irregular Past Tense Use the words to make a sentence in the past tense. Be sure to use correct capitalization and punctuation.

    EXAMPLE: my teacher / wear / glasses
    My teacher wore glasses.

1. we / sit / at little desks

_____

(Continued)

2. there / be / a lot of toys in the room

   _____

3. the teacher / read / books to us

   _____

4. we / go / outside to play

   _____

5. we / have / fun

   _____

Your Name _____   Quiz: Unit 3, Chapter 6

Instructor's Name _____   Date _____

Part A. *To* and *-ing*   Circle the correct verb form to complete each sentence.

EXAMPLE: I decided ((to play) / playing) soccer with a friend.

1. I need (to study / studying) more.

2. I finished (to do / doing) my homework at 10:00 last night.

3. He quit (to smoke / smoking) last year.

4. She enjoys (to take / taking) long walks.

5. They plan (to study / studying) more about computers.

6. She agreed (to play / playing) the piano.

7. They want (to go / going) home now.

8. Do you mind (close / closing) the door?

Part B. Sentence Completion   Complete the following sentences.

EXAMPLE: I'm not _____at home_____.

1. My teacher isn't _____.

2. I didn't go _____.

3. I don't like _____.

4. I was not _____.

5. I didn't _____.

6. I don't want _____.

(Continued)

Part C. Sentence Word Order Write the words in correct sentence order.

    EXAMPLE: Oskar / math / in high school / disliked
    Oskar disliked math in high school.

1. video games / loved / he / playing

   _____

2. wanted / he / to travel / around the world

   _____

3. she / wanted / good grades / to get

   _____

4. to watch / loved / MTV / they

   _____

5. going to / physical education class / disliked / he

   _____

6. enjoyed / meeting / I / new classmates

   _____

Your Name _____   **Quiz: Unit 4, Chapter 7**

Instructor's Name _____   Date _____

Part A. Question Words   Write the missing question word in the following dialogues.

EXAMPLE: ___Where___ did he go? He went *to work*.

1. _____ did she come? She came *at 10:00*.
2. _____ came late? *She* came late.
3. _____ does he work? He works *to pay for rent and food*.
4. _____ do they come to work? They take *the bus*.
5. _____ does it take? It takes *twenty minutes*.

Part B. Writing Comprehension Questions   Read the story and write questions.

> Iselda comes from Mexico City. Now she lives in Chicago. She works at a hospital. She studies ESL at City College. She goes to class four nights a week. She does her homework on the bus. She's a busy woman.

EXAMPLE: Where ___does___ Iselda ___come___ from?

1. Where _____ she _____ now?
2. Where _____ she _____?
3. Where _____ she _____?
4. How often _____ she _____ to class?
5. Where _____ she _____ her homework?

(Continued)

Part C. Writing Questions Write five questions for your instructor to answer.

1. _____
2. _____
3. _____
4. _____
5. _____

Your Name _____ Quiz: Unit 4, Chapter 8

Instructor's Name _____ Date _____

Part A. Subject and Object Pronouns Complete each sentence with the correct subject or object pronoun.

1. *John* is a teacher. _____ teaches at a college.

2. *The students* are very motivated. _____ want to learn everything very fast.

3. John gives *his students* a lot of homework. He wants _____ to study out of class, too.

4. The students respect *their teacher*. They respect _____.

5. The teacher respects *his students*. He respects _____.

6. Yesterday I got *my paycheck*. _____ was bigger than my last one.

7. Our company gave *all of the workers* overtime pay. Our company gave _____ overtime pay for each holiday.

8. I want to take *my girlfriend* out to the movies. I want to take _____ out to dinner, too.

9. *My grandparents* had a store. _____ sold fresh food.

10. *The store* was very popular. _____ was the only store in our neighborhood with homemade food.

Part B. Editing for Pronouns Find four pronoun mistakes in the following paragraphs and correct them.

Samuel

Samuel is a chef at a famous restaurant. Every Saturday, Samuel prepares dinner for over two hundred people. She cooks creative and delicious dinners for they. They often come into the kitchen to meet he.

Samuel doesn't work on Mondays. Him stays at home and orders pizza.

(Continued)

Part C. Editing for Time Order Read the following sentences. Write them again in the correct time order.

Then she has dinner with a friend or her boyfriend.

By 8:00 she is at her computer drinking coffee and answering email.

She usually gets up before the sun gets up.

She tries to close her office door in the afternoons to work on projects.

She exercises, showers, and dresses for work.

She often doesn't leave her desk for lunch.

She gets home just in time to go to bed.

Her morning hours are full of meetings.

She jumps out of bed, has a banana, and goes to her exercise club.

Sometimes she doesn't leave the office until 7:00 or 8:00 P.M.

Molly Sanchez is the president of a small software company. _____

_____
_____
_____
_____
_____
_____
_____

Quiz: Unit 4, Chapter 8 (Concluded)

Your Name _____ Quiz: Unit 5, Chapter 9

Instructor's Name _____ Date _____

Part A. Present Continuous Tense Complete the following sentences with the present continuous form of the verb. Some sentences are negative.

   EXAMPLE: I <u>'m not working</u> today. (not work)

1. I _____ at a concert. (sing)

2. She _____ in a famous restaurant. (cook)

3. They _____ to Hawaii. (travel)

4. We _____ fishing. (not go)

5. You _____ soccer. (not play)

6. He _____ to sew. (learn)

7. It _____. (not rain)

8. I _____ a new car. (not buy)

9. They _____ to music. (listening)

10. Are you _____ an interesting book? (read)

Part B. Possessive Adjectives Fill in the blanks with the correct possessive adjective.

   EXAMPLE: I own a car. It's <u>my</u> car.

1. He has a horse. I learned to ride on _____ horse.

2. They have three children. _____ children have good manners.

3. I have a cat. I love _____ cat very much.

4. She drives a red sports car. Everyone looks at _____ car on the road.

5. We have a family recipe for cheesecake. Would you like _____ recipe?

(Continued)

Part C. Pronouns and Possessive Adjectives Circle the correct pronoun or possessive adjective to complete the paragraph.

> The Tanakas love to spend their free time at home. On weekends they like to spend time in (they, them, their) house. Mariko always has interesting stories to tell (they, them, their), and Tomoyo plays (she, her) favorite songs on the piano. Mr. Tanaka often says, "These are (I, me, my) favorite days. I love spending time with (we, us, our)."

Your Name _____   Quiz: Unit 5, Chapter 10

Instructor's Name _____   Date _____

Part A. Demonstrative Adjectives: *This, That* Write a sentence with the correct demonstrative adjective.

    EXAMPLE: I am writing with a pen. It is my favorite pen.
        This is my favorite pen.

1. The house is around the corner. It is big and white.
   _____

2. The picture is in my hand. It is beautiful.
   _____

3. The movie is playing downtown. It is a horror movie.
   _____

4. The radio is in my sister's room. It is broken.
   _____

5. I have a piece of cake. It is delicious.
   _____

6. The computers in this lab are PCs.
   _____

7. The desks in that classroom are uncomfortable.
   _____

8. The paintings in that room are incredible.
   _____

Part B. Demonstrative Adjectives: *These, Those* Write a sentence with the correct demonstrative adjective.

    EXAMPLE: The computers in this lab are Macs.
        These computers are Macs.

(Continued)

1. The students in the next class are noisy.
   _____

2. The teachers at this school are good.
   _____

3. The dancers in the ballet I saw last night were wonderful.
   _____

4. The stories in that book are very interesting.
   _____

5. The cookies on this plate are delicious.
   _____

Part C. Answering Questions for Prewriting Fill out the following chart about your favorite hobby or sport.

What's your favorite hobby or sport?	
How often do you do this?	
Where do you do it?	
Do you do it alone or with other people?	
Why do you do it?	

Part D. Writing About Your Hobby or Sport Use the chart in Part C to write five sentences about your favorite hobby or sport.

1. _____
2. _____
3. _____
4. _____
5. _____

Your Name _____   Quiz: Unit 6, Chapter 11

Instructor's Name _____   Date _____

Part A. Present Perfect Tense Form: Regular Verbs Complete the following sentences with the correct form of the present perfect tense.

EXAMPLE: I ___have___ often ___watched___ the sun rise.

1. She _____ never _____ another country. (visit)

2. They _____ never _____ on a country road at night. (walk)

3. She _____ _____ for six years without a vacation. (work)

4. We _____ _____ about his problems many times. (talk)

5. I _____ never _____ at another student's paper during a test. (look)

Part B. Present Perfect Tense Answers Answer the following questions with short answers.

EXAMPLE: Have you ever been to Hawaii?
Yes, I have. or No, I haven't.

1. Have you ever been to the Statue of Liberty in New York?
   _____

2. Has your mother ever studied English?
   _____

3. Have you ever jumped out of an airplane?
   _____

4. Has your teacher ever visited your country?
   _____

5. Have you ever danced under the stars?
   _____

(Continued)

Part C. Capitalization and Punctuation Edit the following paragraph for capitalization and punctuation.

> ### john's vacation
>
> last year john took a long vacation. he drove across the united states. have you ever done that It was a very exciting trip. he stopped in small towns and big cities. one of his favorite stops was new orleans. that city is famous for jazz and good food

Your Name _____   **Quiz: Unit 6, Chapter 12**

Instructor's Name _____   Date _____

Part A. Would Rather Answer the following questions.

>   **EXAMPLE:** Would you rather go to a movie or go out to dinner?
>   *I'd rather go to a movie.*

1. Would you rather take a long trip by plane or by car?

   _____

2. Would you rather go out to eat at a friend's house or at a restaurant?

   _____

3. Would you rather have a dog or a cat for a pet?

   _____

Now write two questions using the same pattern.

4. _____?

5. _____?

Part B. Can/Can't Write five sentences with the following words.

>   **EXAMPLE:** I can
>   *I can write English well now.*

1. I can't _____.

2. A baby can't _____.

3. Everybody can _____.

4. Nobody can _____.

5. I can _____.

(Continued)

Part C. Editing for Tense Correct the mistakes in verb tense in the following paragraph. Cross out the mistakes and write the correct forms above.

EXAMPLE: We ~~finish~~ *finished* Chapter 11.

Vacation Anyone?

Alaska is a beautiful place to visit. I goed there last year with my family. We traveling by airplane and boat. We seeing so many beautiful sights and interesting people. It weren't even cold! I plan to visit again some day.

Now we are traveling around Hawaii. This week we stay on the Island of Oahu. There being so many tourists here! We enjoy the beaches and the food. Everything was so colorful. It is a beautiful place to visit. Has you ever been there?

Writing to Learn
THE SENTENCE

UNIT ONE
CHAPTER 1

Myself and Others

A Prewriting

Exercise 1. Telling stories Look at each picture. Read each sentence.

My story

Hello. I am Manuel.
I speak Spanish.
I study English.
I need English!

I speak English at work.
I speak Spanish at home.

I speak English with my new friends.
I like my new language.

Manuel tells Tran's story

This is Tran. She speaks Vietnamese.
She uses English.
She needs English.

She speaks English at work.
She speaks English at home.
She speaks English with friends.

She loves English!

Manuel tells Yoshi's story

This is Yoshi. He speaks Japanese.
He studies English.
He likes English.

He doesn't speak English at work.
He doesn't speak English at home.

He needs English!

Exercise 2. Writing sentences Do not look back at Tran's story. Circle the correct sentence from each group. Then write the sentence under the correct picture.

1. I speak Spanish at home. / She speaks Vietnamese. / He speaks Japanese.

2. She needs English. / He needs English. / I need English.

3. He doesn't speak English at work. / She speaks English at work.

4. She speaks English at home. / I speak Spanish at home. / He doesn't speak English at home.

5. I speak English with my new friends. / She speaks English with friends.

6. He likes English. / She loves English! / He needs English!

Tran's Story

This is Tran.

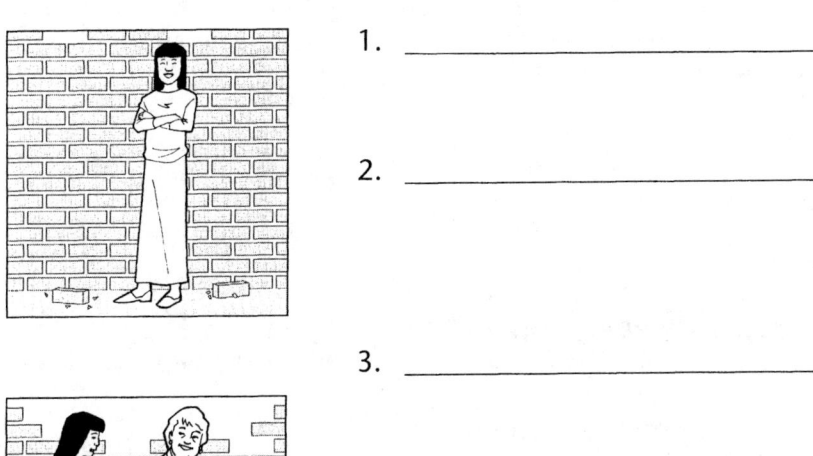

1. _____

2. _____

3. _____

4. _____

5. _____

6. _____

Chapter 1

Exercise 3. Introduce yourself   Your teacher will read these questions. Repeat.

What's your name?

What country do you come from? / What country are you from?

What language do you speak?

Now form two lines: A and B. Students A face students B. Your teacher will call out a word, for example, *country*. Student A will ask Student B the question. Student B will answer. Next Student B will ask the question and Student A will answer. Move to a new partner for the next question.

EXAMPLE: Teacher: country

Student A: What country do you come from?

Student B: I come from Spain. What country do you come from?

Student A: I come from Colombia.

Exercise 4. Alphabet line up   Stand up. Put yourself in alphabetical order (A, B, C, D, and so on) by your first name. Each person says his or her name loudly and clearly. Everyone will listen. Make sure everyone is in the right order.
Now put yourself in alphabetical order by your last name.

B Structure

Exercise 1. Manuel's story: Identifying subjects and verbs   In Manuel's story, underline the subjects with one line and the verbs with two lines.

EXAMPLE: I come from Columbia.

Manuel's Story

My name is Manuel. I speak Spanish. I study English. I need English! I speak English at work. I speak Spanish at home. I speak English with my new friends. I like my new language.

Subjects and Verbs

Every sentence has a subject and verb. The subject tells us who or what is doing or experiencing something. The verb tells us what the subject is doing or experiencing.

EXAMPLE: I   come   from China.
              subject   *verb*

Exercise 2. Tran's story and Yoshi's story: Writing verbs Finish Tran's story and finish Yoshi's story. Write the verbs in the blank spaces. Use *speak, need, use,* and *like*.

Verb Forms

In the simple present tense, the third person singular (he, she, it) form of regular verbs needs an **-s**.

I	come	we	come
you	come	you	come
he/she/it	come**s**	they	come

Tran's Story

This is Tran. She speaks Vietnamese. She _____ English. She _____ English at work. She _____ English at home. She _____ English with friends. She _____ English!

Yoshi's Story

This is Yoshi. He _____ Japanese. He _____ English. He _____ English. He _____ English at work. He _____ English at home. He _____ English!

Chapter 1

Exercise 3. Identifying ourselves: Verb forms Write the correct verb forms in these sentences.

1. They _____ from South America. (come)

2. He _____ Portuguese. (speak)

3. I _____ languages. (like)

4. My friend _____ English. (need)

5. You _____ Spanish and English. (speak)

6. She _____ French. (love)

C Writing and Editing

Exercise 1. Why do you study English? Put a check mark (✓) next to what is true for *you*. I study English . . .

❏ for work ❏ for my future

❏ for my children ❏ for my parents

❏ to travel ❏ to find a friend

❏ to make new friends ❏ (Add your ideas) _____

Write down each sentence that you checked.

EXAMPLE: I study English for work.

_____
_____
_____
_____
_____
_____
_____

Each person reads the sentences that he or she wrote.

 **Exercise 2. Your story** Draw pictures of your story. Write sentences under the pictures.

My Story

Basic Capitalization Rules

- Every sentence always begins with a capital letter.
    EXAMPLE: **T**his country is very big.

- The word *I* is always capitalized.
    EXAMPLE: My classmate and **I** walk to class.

- People's names are always capitalized.
    EXAMPLE: Today I worked with **E**lvia, **V**ladimir, and **A**ki.

- Languages (for example, English, Russian), countries (for example, Canada, Australia), and people from countries (for example, Korean, French) are always capitalized.
    EXAMPLE: Some **C**anadians speak **E**nglish as a first language and some people from **C**anada speak **F**rench.

> ## Basic Punctuation Rule
>
> Every sentence ends with a period (.), an exclamation mark (!), or a question mark (?)

Exercise 3. Editing practice Correct the following sentences. Add capital letters and punctuation.

EXAMPLE: my teacher speaks english and spanish
My teacher speaks English and Spanish.

1. people in haiti speak french

2. where does he come from

3. many people in canada speak two languages

4. she and I are partners today

5. what city do you come from

Exercise 4. More editing practice Correct the following pairs of sentences. Add capital letters and punctuation.

EXAMPLE: jessica comes from taiwan albert comes from france
Jessica comes from Taiwan. Albert comes from France.

1. one classmate comes from korea one classmate comes from spain

2. our teacher speaks english clearly I always understand

3. the student from japan works in a mexican restaurant the student from guatemala works in a japanese sushi restaurant

4. the ukraine is different from russia ukranians speak a different language too

5. iranians do not speak arabic what language do iranians speak

6. brazilians don't speak spanish brazilians speak portuguese

7. how many languages do you speak I speak two languages

D Journal Assignment

Buy a notebook with lines on the paper. This is your journal. You will write in it. Your teacher will read your journal. Your journal is a place to write different things.

Here is your first journal assignment.

- Listen for names. Read names. Write down the names of classmates. Write down the names of streets. Write down the names of buildings on your campus or near your school. Make lists of different kinds of names. Copy the spelling. Or try to spell the name yourself.

UNIT ONE
CHAPTER 2

Myself and Others

A Prewriting

Exercise 1. Telling stories Read these statements. Look at the pictures. Write the correct sentences under each picture.

He makes new friends.   He breaks down the wall.
He lives with a family.   He talks to people everywhere.
He studies in the computer lab.   He speaks in class.

Yoshi learns. He breaks down the wall.

Exercise 2. Retell the story You are Yoshi. Begin the story with **I.** Tell the whole story. Try not to look at the sentences. Just look at the pictures on page 12.

EXAMPLE: I learn. I break down the wall.

Exercise 3. How do you learn English? Put a check mark next to each sentence that is true for *you*.

- ❏ I speak in class.
- ❏ I watch television in English.
- ❏ I listen to music in English.
- ❏ I talk to people.
- ❏ I study at home.
- ❏ I practice English on the computer.
- ❏ I live with an American family.
- ❏ Other _____

Exercise 4. How do your friends learn English? Interview a classmate. Find out how he or she learns English. Use the sentences in the picture story and Exercise 3. Ask questions.

EXAMPLE:
Questions to classmate	Classmate's answer
What's your name?	Min.
Min, do you speak in class?	Yes.

Write in your book: ___Min makes new friends___

Ask more questions. Write down the answers.

_____

_____

_____

_____

Chapter 2

Exercise 5. A poem about learning English Read the poem silently. Listen to your teacher read it. Now read it with a classmate. You read one line. Your classmate reads the next line.

Learning English

There is a wall of language between me and you

I must break it down

Tell me what to do

What comes first? Words, grammar, sounds?

Help me make this wall come down

Exercise 6. What I can do Read the poem again. Next make a list of some words from the poem that you know.

Words _____

_____

Write two sentences you know how to write.

Sentences _____

_____

_____

_____

Write some words you can say well. _____

_____

_____

B Structure

Singular Subjects and Plural Subjects

A singular subject is one subject.

EXAMPLE: **Yoshi** studies in the language lab.

He studies at home.

A plural subject is more than one subject.

EXAMPLE: **Yoshi and Maria** study English at night.

Many students study English.

Exercise 1. Identifying singular and plural subjects. Put an **S** next to singular subjects and a **P** next to plural subjects.

_____ 1. Maria speaks English at work at the hospital.

_____ 2. Maria and her mother don't speak English to each other.

_____ 3. The boys know English from playing basketball.

_____ 4. She likes learning with a computer.

_____ 5. They need English for their jobs.

_____ 6. My teacher speaks three languages.

_____ 7. Your friends want to study here, too.

_____ 8. We practice speaking in the cafeteria.

_____ 9. It is not easy to learn a new language.

_____ 10. The class tries to speak English all of the time.

Spelling of verbs that end in -y

Notice that the verb **study** ends in **-y.** Verbs that end in **-y** change to **-ies** for he, she, and it. If a vowel (a, e, i, o, u) comes before **y,** there is no change.

EXAMPLE: I study English.

Maria stud**ies** English.

She stud**ies** English.

EXAMPLE: I buy milk at the store.

Ko buy**s** milk at the store.

He buy**s** milk at the store.

Here are some common verbs that end in **-y.**

| say | cry | hurry | lay | worry |
| try | fry | rely | marry | pay |

Exercise 2. Who studies? Write the correct form of the verb **study.**

1. Maria _____ in the lab.

2. Maria and her mother _____ at home.

3. The boys _____ at work.

4. She _____ in her room.

5. They _____ on the bus.

6. My teacher _____ in his office.

7. Your friends _____ at school.

8. We _____ in the cafeteria.

9. You _____ in the library.

10. The class _____ in the classroom.

Write down the places where *you* study.

_____

_____

_____

Now tell a classmate where you study.

Exercise 3. Writing verbs that end in -y Write each verb that ends in **-y** from the box on page 16. Use the name **Ali** as the subject. Be careful. Some verbs change to **-ies.** Some verbs do not change.

EXAMPLE: Ali says . . .

1. _____   6. _____
2. _____   7. _____
3. _____   8. _____
4. _____   9. _____
5. _____   10. _____

Exercise 4. Interview with a classmate Ask a classmate these questions. Write down **yes** or **no.**

Classmate's name: _____

Do you try to speak English all the time? _____

Do you cry at sad movies? _____

Do you hurry when you are late to class? _____

Do you pay your bills? _____

Do you worry about things? _____

Chapter 2

Now write sentences for all the **yes** answers.

EXAMPLE: Do you cry at sad movies? *(yes)*
Jose cries at sad movies.

_____
_____
_____
_____

C Writing and Editing

Exercise 1. Writing new sentences   Read each sentence from Yoshi's story. Write a second sentence.

EXAMPLE: Yoshi learns fast. / he-study-hard
He studies hard.

1. Yoshi makes new friends. / he-meet-them-every day

_____

2. Yoshi talks to people everywhere. / he-speak-to them-in English

_____

3. Yoshi speaks in class. / he-talk-to his classmates

_____

4. Yoshi studies in the computer lab. / he-use-the Internet

_____

5. Yoshi lives with a family. / he-eat-dinner-with them

_____

6. Yoshi breaks down the wall. / he-understand-people-better

_____

**Exercise 2. Writing sentences about yourself** Look at the sentences you just wrote in Exercise 1. Rewrite each sentence that is true for *you*.

EXAMPLE: Yoshi understands people better.
I understand people better.

_____
_____
_____
_____
_____
_____

Exercise 3. Rewriting sentences using *and* Look at the sentences you wrote in Exercise 2. Write two of them together using **and**.

EXAMPLE: I understand people better. / I talk to people everywhere.
I understand people better, and I talk to people everywhere.

_____
_____
_____

**Exercise 4. Compare your sentences** Read your sentences one at a time to your partner. Listen to your partner's sentences. Are they the same as yours?

D Journal Assignment

Think about what you do every day. Write down the things you do.

EXAMPLE: I take the bus every day.

UNIT TWO
CHAPTER 3

Family and Relationships

A Prewriting

Exercise 1. Matching Each sentence matches a picture. Put the number of the picture next to the sentence.

_____ a. I was the first child born in my family.

_____ b. My mother and father got married in a church.

_____ c. I have two brothers and a sister.

_____ d. I am an aunt.

_____ e. I have nieces and nephews.

_____ f. My parents are grandparents now.

_____ g. My family always ate dinner together.

_____ h. My mother and father fell in love.

_____ i. I was born in a hospital.

_____ j. My mother had three children after me.

_____ k. My family is close.

_____ l. My family began with my mother and father.

1.

2.

3.

4.

Exercise 2. My life Rewrite the sentences from Exercise 1. Write only the ones that are true for *you*.

    EXAMPLE: I was born in a hospital.

Write each sentence after the other one.

    EXAMPLE: I was born in a hospital. I was the first child born in my family.

_____

_____

_____

_____

_____

_____

_____

_____

Exercise 3. Talking to a classmate Read your sentences from Exercise 2 to a classmate. Read them one at a time. Then ask your classmate a question.

    EXAMPLE: I was born in a hospital. Were you born in a hospital?

                I was the first child born in my family. Were you the first child born in your family?

Write your classmate's answers below. Then switch roles.

_____

_____

_____

_____

_____

Chapter 3

Exercise 4. Writing about your family Look at the words below. They are from the picture story on page 20. Try to write a sentence using each word. Write about yourself and your own family. Write five sentences.

mother　father　child　family　sister　nephew
brother　niece　aunt　grandparents　children

EXAMPLE: (children) I have three children.

1. _____
2. _____
3. _____
4. _____
5. _____

B Structure

Exercise 1. The verb *be*—present and past Read each sentence. Is the verb *be* in the present or past tense? Write **PR** for present. Write **P** for past. Use the chart on page 23 if you need help.

EXAMPLE: __P__ I was a good child. (**P** is for past tense. **Was** is a past tense form of **be**.)

____ 1. I am a mother.

____ 2. I was in high school.

____ 3. You were at school.

____ 4. They are friends.

____ 5. You are a good person.

____ 6. She is my sister.

____ 7. He was my teacher.

____ 8. We were in the library.

____ 9. It was a great party.

____ 10. We are students.

The Verb Be: Present and Past

Present Tense of **be**	Past Tense of **be**
I am	I was
you are	you were
he/she/it is	he/she/it was
we are	we were
you are	you were
they are	they were

Exercise 2. Writing sentences with *be* Look at the words below. Make sentences with five of these words. Use the verb **be**. Use present tense or past tense.

EXAMPLES: (baby) I was a good baby.
(student) I am a college student.

brother	girl
baby	father
sister	child
boy	friend
mother	student

1. _____
2. _____
3. _____
4. _____
5. _____

Some Common Verbs—Present Tense

get	go	have	do
I get	I go	I have	I do
you get	you go	you have	you do
he/she/it gets	he/she/it goes	he/she/it has	he/she/it does
we get	we go	we have	we do
you get	you go	you have	you do
they get	they go	they have	they do

Exercise 3. Using be, get, go, have, do Complete each sentence. Use a form of **be, get, go, have,** or **do.** Use the present tense.

EXAMPLE: He ___gets___ a letter from his mother once a week.

1. I _____ 24 years old.

2. She _____ two brothers.

3. He _____ English class every day.

4. They _____ to class in the morning.

5. You _____ your homework at night.

6. We _____ our pay on Friday.

7. I _____ home after class.

8. You _____ the bus near school.

9. We _____ friends.

10. She _____ well in English class.

Exercise 4: Rewriting sentences Rewrite each sentence in Exercise 3. Use **I** as the subject.

>   **EXAMPLE:** He gets a letter from his mother once a week.
>   *I get a letter from my mother once a week.*

You may change the sentence to make it true for you.

>   **EXAMPLE:** I get a phone call from my mother once a week. *or*
>   I never get a phone call from my mother.

1. _____
2. _____
3. _____
4. _____
5. _____
6. _____
7. _____
8. _____
9. _____
10. _____

Exercise 5. Group dictation Each person dictates two sentences from Exercise 4 to the group. The other students write. Then check your answers.

1. _____
2. _____
3. _____
4. _____
5. _____
6. _____
7. _____
8. _____

Writing and Editing

Exercise 1. Editing for usage Read the story. Pay attention to the verbs. Circle the correct words to complete the story. Then check your story with a classmate.

EXAMPLE: I (am, (was)) born in Mexico.

My Life

I (am, was) born in Taiwan. I (have, has) a brother and a sister. I (is, am) the youngest of three children. Now I (am, was) 21 years old. I (are, am) a student of English. I (do, have) three English classes every day. I (get, gets) help with English from my friend. Her name (are, is) Anna. She (go, goes) to school, too. She (have, has) Chinese classes. I (help, helps) her with her Chinese.

Exercise 2. Word order Write the words in the correct order to make a sentence.

EXAMPLE: born / he / in Russia / was
He was born in Russia.

1. she / in Canada / now / lives

_____

2. 22 years old / he / is / now

_____

3. of six children / the oldest / is / he

_____

4. studies / English / he

_____

5. every day / has / he / two classes

_____

6. homework / he / gets / every night

_____

Exercise 3. Sentence order   Read the sentences. Which sentence is first for a story? Which sentence is next? Write numbers next to the sentences.

Then they had me.

I have three sisters.

I have two children.

My mother and father got married in a temple.

I am the oldest child.

Now I am married.

Now write the sentences in order.

_____
_____
_____
_____
_____

Exercise 4. Write your story   Look at the picture story on page 20 again. Then read Exercise 2 on page 26 again. Now write your own story below. Write about yourself. Write about your family.

_____
_____
_____
_____
_____

Exercise 5. We are the same. We are different. Read your story. Listen to your classmate's story. Maybe your classmate's story is the same as your story. Put a check mark next to the sentence that is the same for your classmate.

Now go around the classroom. Read your story. Find sentences that are the same for you *and* for your classmate. Add **and** to connect two sentences. Use **too** to show two things are the same. Now write about those sentences.

EXAMPLE: I am the oldest child, and Helen is the oldest child, too.

_____

_____

_____

_____

_____

D Journal Assignment

Find out about another family, for example, your classmate's family, your homestay family, or your teacher's family. Ask questions about the family. Write down what you find out.

UNIT TWO
CHAPTER 4
Family and Relationships

A Prewriting

Exercise 1. Discover the story There are three sentences for each picture on page 31. Write the two sentences that are correct for each picture.

1. Carol was a single mother.

   Carol had a baby.

   Carol and her family enjoyed walking in the park.

2. Carol worked as a security guard.

   Carol went shopping.

   Carol worked at a mall.

3. Carol's mother takes care of the boys.

   Carol's husband is home.

   The younger boy is having a snack.

4. Carol works in the college bookstore.

   Carol studies at home.

   Carol is sitting in class.

1. _____

2. _____

3. _____

4. _____

Chapter 4

Exercise 2. Carol is. Carol isn't. The negative of **is** is **is not**. **Is not** is often contracted (made shorter) to **isn't**. Read the list of words below. Then write sentences about Carol. Use **is** or **isn't**.

    EXAMPLE: teacher
            Carol isn't a teacher.

1. student
   _____

2. mother
   _____

3. grandmother
   _____

4. bookstore clerk
   _____

5. security guard
   _____

6. wife
   _____

7. woman
   _____

8. husband
   _____

Exercise 3. What were you?   Think of your past. What were you? A high school student? A worker? A football player? Write down what you were in the past.

EXAMPLE: I was a football player.

_____

_____

_____

_____

Now read your sentences to a classmate.

Exercise 4. What are you?   Think of the present. What are you now? Write down what you are now.

EXAMPLE: Now I am a student.

_____

_____

_____

_____

Now read your sentences to a classmate.

B Structure

Exercise 1. *Years ago* and *now*   **Years ago** is a time in the past. **Now** is the present time. Fill out this chart. Write a sentence in each box. Write the truth.

	Years ago	**Now**
have money	Years ago, I did not have money.	Now I have a little money.
be in elementary school		
have a lot of friends		
get sick a lot		
do homework		
go to work after school		
have problems		
be happy		
do well in primary school		
get good grades		
go to class every day		

Negatives and Contractions: I

Here are the negative forms of the verbs, **be, do, get, go,** and **have** in present and past tense with **I.**

Present Tense

be	do	get	go	have
I am not	I do not do	I do not get	I do not go	I do not have
I'm not	I don't do	I don't get	I don't go	I don't have

Past Tense

be	do	get	go	have
I was not	I did not do	I did not get	I did not go	I did not have
I wasn't	I didn't do	I didn't get	I didn't go	I didn't have

Exercise 2. Complete the sentence Use your own words to complete the sentence. Take turns. Do the exercise two times.

> **EXAMPLE:** I wasn't
> I wasn't very good at speaking English last year.

1. I didn't do _____

2. I didn't have _____

3. I wasn't _____

4. I didn't go _____

5. I didn't get _____

Exercise 3. Interview a classmate Use the verbs from Exercises 1 and 2 above. Write down five questions. Interview your classmate about his or her life. Then write his or her answer to each question.

> **EXAMPLES:** Were you a soccer player?
> Yes, I was a soccer player.

1. Question: _____

   Answer: _____

2. Question: _____

   Answer: _____

3. Question: _____

   Answer: _____

4. Question: _____

   Answer: _____

5. Question: _____

   Answer: _____

Exercise 4. Writing *he* or *she* Read your answers from Exercise 3 again. Rewrite the answers using **he** or **she**. Use the Negatives and Contractions Box for help.

Negatives and Contractions: He, She, and It

Here are the negative forms of the verbs, **be, do, get, go,** and **have** in present and past tense with **he. She** and **it** are the same as **he.**

Present Tense

be	do	get	go	have
He is not	He does not do	He does not get	He does not go	He does not have
He's not	He doesn't do	He doesn't get	He doesn't go	He doesn't have

Past Tense

be	do	get	go	have
He was not	He did not do	He did not get	He did not go	He did not have
He wasn't	He didn't do	He didn't get	He didn't go	He didn't have

EXAMPLE: Q: Ahmed, did you do well in primary school?

A: Yes, I did.

He did well in primary school.

Unit 2: Family and Relationships

1. _____
2. _____
3. _____
4. _____
5. _____

C Writing and Editing

Exercise 1. Editing for past tense and negative Read the story. Pay attention to past tense. Pay attention to the negative of verbs. Cross out the mistakes. Write in the correct answers.

                          did
EXAMPLE: Last year I ~~do~~ not study English.

> Last year I am a cook in a restaurant. I did have not English classes. I got depressed. My job has no future. So now I go to an English class after work. I have not problems learning English. It is fun! I do well in class!

Exercise 2. Editing for present tense, past tense, and negative Read the story. Pay attention to the tense. It can be present. It can be past. Pay attention to the negative of verbs. Cross out mistakes. Write in the correct answers.

                        am
EXAMPLE: I ~~was~~ not a full-time cook now.

> These days I had English classes during the morning. In the afternoon, I not have class. I had a job. I am a clerk in the college bookstore. I was happy now! I do get not depressed. I went to school with a smile on my face. I don't worry!

Chapter 4

Exercise 3. Reviewing time order The sentences below are part of a story. The story needs to be put in the correct order. Read the story. Rewrite the sentences below the story.

> My children are in school now. I worked full-time. I go to school now. I didn't go to school. I got divorced. My mother took care of my children. I got married and had two children. My mother takes care of them after school. I work after class.

_____

_____

_____

_____

_____

D Journal Assignment

Write two sentences each day in your journal. Write one sentence about the past. Write one sentence about the present.

Education

 Prewriting

Exercise 1. Match the sentence with the picture This is Pedro's story. He is in each picture of the story on page 41. Write the sentences under the correct picture. Each picture has three sentences.

1. My preschool teacher smiled a lot.
2. I didn't like math class.
3. I played with cars.
4. Our math teacher wore glasses.
5. There wasn't a blackboard in our classroom.
6. We sat on chairs at tables.
7. I read a lot in class.
8. I sat next to my girlfriend.
9. There weren't desks in our classroom.
10. Our English instructor doesn't speak my language.
11. Every student pays attention to the teacher.
12. I practice English with my classmates.

1.

_____
_____
_____

2.

_____
_____
_____

3.

_____
_____
_____

4.

_____
_____
_____

Exercise 2. Vocabulary hunt Look at the pictures in Exercise 1 again. How many vocabulary words do you know for each picture? Write down all the words you know from each picture in the boxes below.

1.
toys

2.

3.

4.

Exercise 3. Word dictation Say a word from Box 1 in Exercise 2. Ask your partner to write that word. Next your partner says a word from Box 1. You write it down. Then continue with boxes 2, 3, and 4.

1. _____ 3. _____

2. _____ 4. _____

Now look at your partner's words and let your partner look at your words. Decide about spelling. Who is correct? Are you both correct? Do the activity again.

1. _____ 3. _____

2. _____ 4. _____

Exercise 4. Tell a story First, read the sentences in Exercise 1 again. Then read the words in Exercise 3. Now, in your group, each person tells a story, box by box. The other two people listen.

Unit 3: Education

B Structure

Exercise 1. Regular verbs in past tense Regular verbs in past tense are verbs that end in **-ed**. Read the verbs in the list below and put an **R** next to the regular verbs.

____ 1. wore

____ 2. practiced

____ 3. smiled

____ 4. were

____ 5. did

____ 6. played

____ 7. sat

____ 8. was

____ 9. studied

____ 10. liked

____ 11. read

____ 12. worked

Exercise 2. Present tense to past tense Change each sentence from present to past tense. Write only true sentences. Do not write the past tense sentences that are not true for you.

EXAMPLE: Children play with toys.
I played with toys.

1. My nephew attends preschool.

   I _____

2. He plays with the other children.

   I _____

3. He smiles a lot at his teacher.

   I _____

4. My niece learns poems in elementary school.

   I _____

5. She listens to music in class, too.

   I _____

Chapter 5

6. She likes her teacher.

   I _____

7. My brother studies math in high school.

   I _____

8. He copies homework from his girlfriend.

   I _____

9. He dislikes math class.

   I _____

Now read your sentences to a partner. Explain more about each sentence.

EXAMPLE: I played with toys. My favorite toy was a playhouse.

Exercise 3. Learning irregular past tense verbs Look at the list of irregular past tense verbs that follows these verbs. Match them with the present tense.

Past Tense	Present Tense
____ 1. wrote	a. are
____ 2. sat	b. sit
____ 3. had	c. wear
____ 4. read	d. go
____ 5. wore	e. do
____ 6. went	f. have
____ 7. got	g. read
____ 8. did	h. write
____ 9. were	i. get
____ 10. took care of	j. take care of

Unit 3: Education

Exercise 4. Past tense and present tense Read each sentence. Circle the correct tense.

EXAMPLE: I (attended, attend) preschool in the morning.

1. I (went, go) to a preschool near my house.
2. My preschool teacher still (teaches, taught) at my preschool these days.
3. She just (gets, got) married last June.
4. Pati, my high school classmate, (studies, studied) English two years ago at a community college.
5. She (is, was) a medical student now.
6. She (reads, read) her medical books in English.
7. Dora, my high school girlfriend, (sits, sat) at the desk next to me.
8. She (is, was) a wife and a mother now.
9. She (takes care of, took care of) her children at home.
10. Saad (goes, went) to my new school.
11. He (speaks, spoke) some English, not a lot.
12. We (see, saw) each other every day in class.

Exercise 5. Practice with negation Some sentences from Exercise 4 are repeated here in negative form. They are not in the same order. Match each sentence to one in the list on the right side of the page.

EXAMPLE: I didn't go to a preschool near my home.

I went to a preschool far from my home.

1. ___ We don't see each other every day.
2. ___ Saad doesn't go to my new school.
3. ___ She doesn't take care of her children.
4. ___ She didn't get married.
5. ___ Dora didn't sit at the desk next to me.
6. ___ Pati didn't study English.
7. ___ She isn't a medical student.
8. ___ He doesn't speak much English.

a. She sat far away from me.
b. He speaks very little English.
c. She's still single.
d. We hardly ever see each other.
e. She studied Spanish.
f. He goes to my old school.
g. She has a baby-sitter.
h. She is a business major.

C Writing and Editing

Capitalization

- School subjects do not have capital letters: arithmetic, biology, calculus, dance, economics
- Jobs in education do not have capital letters: professor, teacher, instructor, classroom aide
- Job titles have capital letters: Professor Smith, Director of Admissions, President Carter
- Names of languages have capital letters: Albanian, Chinese, English
- Names of schools have capital letters: Near East University, Happy College
- Academic degrees have capital letters: A.A. (Associate of Arts), B.S. (Bachelor of Science), M.B.A., Ph.D.

Punctuation

- Periods are used in abbreviations (shortened forms of words)

    Education Dept.   (Department)   Dr. Nash   (Doctor)
    Prof. Sills   (Professor)   Pres. Young   (President)

Exercise 1. Capitalization and punctuation practice Read each sentence. Write each sentence again and change letters to capital or small. Put in periods.

1. Prof smith came to class late

   _____

2. I study History

   _____

3. My brother studied german

   _____

4. Dr McDoodle has a phd

_____

5. I had trouble with Mathematics and latin in high school

_____

6. Horace got a bs from Ovid college

_____

7. Pres Lee was the chairman of the department of chemical engineering at Eastern county college

_____

_____

8. professor welby was my Instructor for freshman english

_____

Exercise 2. Reading notes Read the notes below. Tell Clara's story.

Preschool	Elementary school
Went far away, cried a lot, learned to draw, sang songs, loved milk and cookies	Learned to read and write, went on field trips, liked my teacher, had a sandwich every day for lunch, wrote love notes to Billy

High school	College
Went to Mountain View High, was a member of the choir, studied Spanish, went on an exchange to Mexico, got my driver's license	Majored in Latin American Studies, took Portuguese and Spanish, learned to play the guitar, met Raul in Santiago, failed calculus

 **Exercise 3. Recalling a story** Look at the pictures to help you tell Clara's story again. Don't look at the notes in Exercise 2. Each person can tell one part of the story. The other students should listen and help.

1.

2.

3.

4.

Each person now changes parts of the story and tells the story again.

Unit 3: Education

Exercise 4. Writing sentences about school Choose one of the boxes in Exercise 2. Write your own sentences about your experience. Use the sentences in the boxes to help you.

EXAMPLE: I learned to read and write in elementary school.

_____
_____
_____
_____
_____

Exercise 5. What was good about it? Think about your experience in school. Write five sentences about things that were good.

EXAMPLE: I liked the food in the cafeteria at my high school.

1. _____
2. _____
3. _____
4. _____
5. _____

Compare your classmate's sentences to your sentences. Are they the same? Are they different? Are they similar?

Copy your sentences on a piece of paper. Put the paper on the classroom wall. Go around and read everyone's sentences.

D Journal Assignment

Talk to someone who is not your classmate. Talk to that person about school. Try to take notes. Write down in your journal what you remember. Tell that person's story in writing.

Education

CHAPTER 6

 **Prewriting**

Exercise 1. Who am I? Check any sentence that is true for *you*.

_____ 1. I am not a teacher.

_____ 2. I do not study English.

_____ 3. I didn't go to elementary school in the United States.

_____ 4. I don't like mathematics.

_____ 5. I don't want to speak English.

_____ 6. I wasn't a good student in high school.

_____ 7. I'm not in class now.

_____ 8. I did not study last night.

_____ 9. I don't speak English.

_____ 10. I was not in the school library yesterday.

Exercise 2. Am I like* Oskar? Read the sentences below. They are about Oskar. Put an **L** next to each sentence for which *you* are like Oskar.

1.

2.

3.

4.

____ 1. Oskar doesn't like to study. He likes to have fun.

____ 2. Oskar didn't learn English in elementary school. He learned German.

____ 3. Oskar does not like to use computers. He likes to use video players.

____ 4. Oskar did not want to study English. He wanted to study Italian.

____ 5. Oskar does not like sitting in English class. He likes hanging out outside.

____ 6. Oskar doesn't want to get a degree. He just wants to learn a little English.

____ 7. Oskar doesn't like to do homework. He likes to play video games.

____ 8. Oskar didn't like to solve math problems. He liked to talk to classmates.

* *Be like* means "be similar in some way."

Chapter 6

Exercise 3. Comparing yourself Use the sentences and pictures in Exercise 2 to compare yourself with Oskar. Make notes below. Make notes on similarities. Make notes on differences.

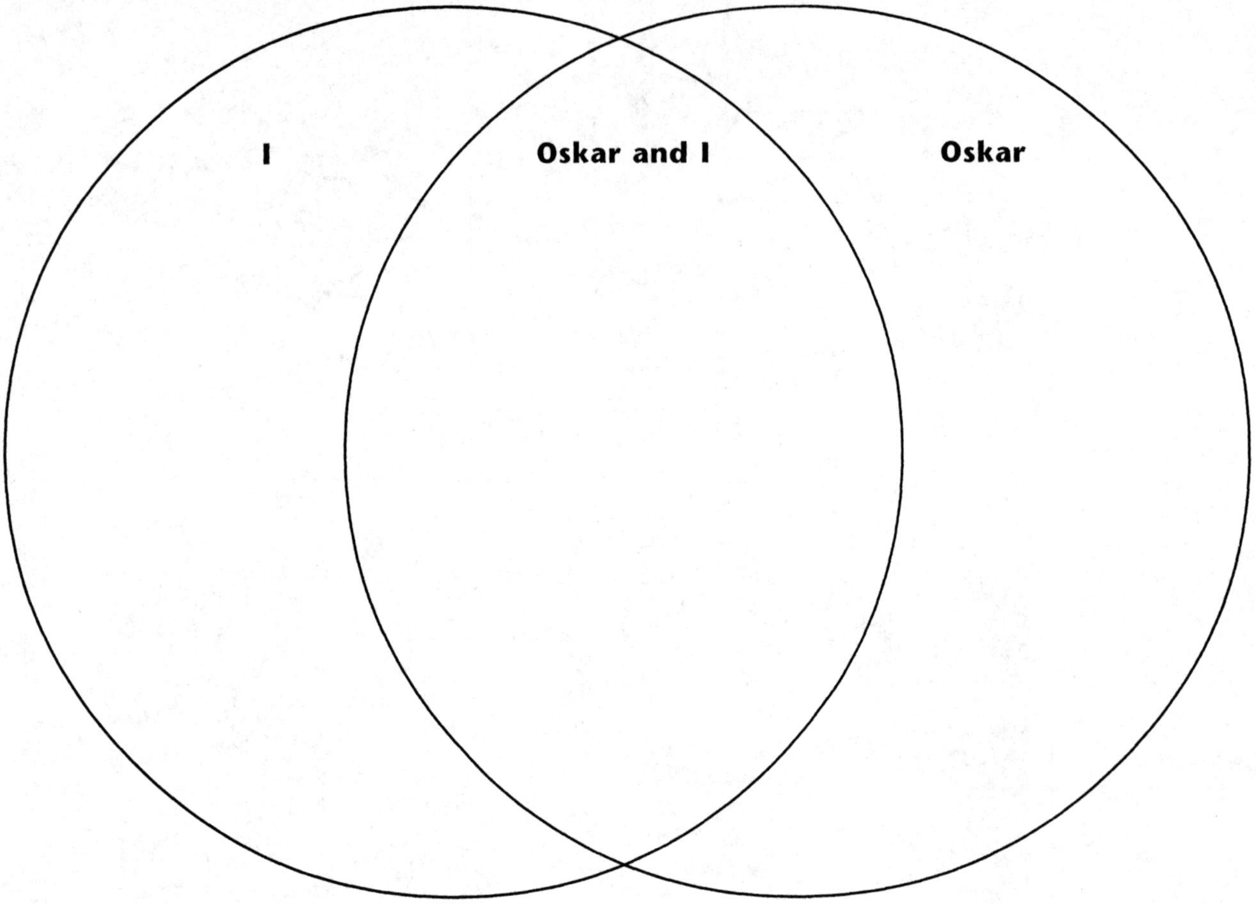

```
        I           Oskar and I        Oskar
```

Now find a partner. Talk to your partner about the similarities and differences between you and Oskar.

Exercise 4. I like. I don't like. First, think about the things you like.

  EXAMPLE: chocolate, friendly dogs, the first snowfall, the beach, bluebirds

Then, think about the things you don't like.

  EXAMPLE: loud people on airplanes, boring teachers, being sick

52

Unit 3: Education

B Structure

Exercise 1. Verb + verb: *Like to, want to* Use the following words to write at least six sentences.

EXAMPLE: study English
I like to study English, and I want to study English.

study computer science
watch movies
write poems
play soccer
attend class
play guitar
go shopping
exercise
listen to music
do homework
(other—your idea)

1. _____
2. _____
3. _____
4. _____
5. _____
6. _____

Exercise 2. Verb + verb: *Like + -ing* After *like* you can use **to + base** form **(to study)** or the **-ing** form **(studying)**. Write the sentences from Exercise 1 again using the **-ing** form with *like.* (Note that you cannot use the **-ing** form with **want.**)

EXAMPLE: I like studying English, and I want to study English.

1. _____
2. _____

Chapter 6

3. _____
4. _____
5. _____
6. _____

Exercise 3. Verb + verb: I don't like studying, but I have to study. In Exercise 1, you talked about things you like doing. You want to do those things. However, sometimes you have to do things you don't like doing. Here are the words from Exercise 1 again. Write at least four negative sentences.

EXAMPLE: I don't like studying English, but I have to study English.

study computer science	attend class	exercise
write poems	play guitar	do homework
watch movies	listen to music	(other—your idea)
play soccer	go shopping	

1. _____
2. _____
3. _____
4. _____

Now add three more sentences of your own. Ask your classmates or teacher for help with vocabulary.

EXAMPLE: I don't like cleaning the bathroom, but I have to clean the bathroom.

1. _____
2. _____
3. _____

Verb + to or -ing

Here is a list of some common English verbs. One column has verbs that use the **to** form (infinitive). The other column has verbs that use the **-ing** form (gerund). Some verbs use both **to** and **-ing**.

To		**-ing**	
want	learn	dislike	keep
need	decide	enjoy	appreciate
have	agree	finish	mind
ask	expect	discuss	quit
plan	refuse	practice	regret

EXAMPLE: I need to study.   **EXAMPLE:** I dislike studying.

Exercise 4. Verb + verb: Using the correct form Circle the appropriate verb form to complete the sentence.

EXAMPLE: He agreed ((to play) / playing) soccer with a friend.

1. Oskar needs (to study / studying) more.

2. Oskar finished (to play / playing) video games at midnight.

3. He expects (to find / finding) a good job.

4. He quit (to smoke / smoking) last year.

5. He enjoys (to talk / talking) with friends.

6. He has (to call / calling) his grandfather.

7. He wants (to buy / buying) a new computer game.

8. He dislikes (to do / doing) homework.

Chapter 6

C Writing and Editing

Exercise 1. Oskar in elementary school   Read the story below. Look closely at the verb + verb combinations **(to, -ing)**. Look at the verb tenses. Circle the correct verb forms.

Oskar in Elementary School

Oskar (goes / went) to elementary school for eight years. He disliked (to study / studying) in school. He (is / was) a very active child. He enjoyed (to play / playing) games, and he enjoyed (to talk / talking) to his classmates. He never wanted (to study / studying). He always wanted (to play / playing) video games. Of course, he had (to study / studying). His parents planned (to send / sending) him to a very good middle school. So he needed (to study / studying). Finally, Oskar decided (to study / studying) a little. He wanted (to make / making) his parents happy.

Exercise 2. Oskar in high school   The words in these sentences are mixed up. Write the sentences in the correct word order.

EXAMPLE: Oskar / studying math / in high school / disliked.
   Oskar disliked studying math in high school.

1. Oskar / Italy / going to / dreamed of

   _____

2. enjoyed / classmates / talking to / Oskar

   _____

3. had / math / to study / Oskar

   _____

Unit 3: Education

4. going to / disliked / Oskar / math class

_____

5. video games / loved / he / playing

_____

6. wanted / he / to travel / in Italy

_____

7. listening to / loved / Oskar / opera

_____

8. needed / to go / to a tutor / Oskar / after school

_____

9. to Italy / his parents / to send / agreed / Oskar

_____

10. he / to get / good grades / needed

_____

Exercise 3. Oskar in English class Now Oskar studies English, not Italian. What happened? Write your ideas after each sentence below.

    EXAMPLE: Oskar decided to become a businessman.

                    He needed _to learn English, the international language of business._

1. Oskar came to the United States. He needs _____

2. Oskar enjoys speaking English to his classmates. He likes _____

3. Oskar decided to make his parents happy. He loves _____

4. Oskar expects to get a job in an international company. He wants _____

Chapter 6

5. Oskar considered studying Italian first.

   _____

6. Oskar needs to become fluent in English.

   _____

7. Oskar misses being with his family.

   _____

8. Oskar refuses to give up his dream of Italy and opera.

   _____

9. Oskar regrets being a poor student in high school.

   _____

10. Oskar loves to dream about the future.

    _____

Exercise 4. Give advice to Oskar You read about Oskar. You know him a little. Write him a short letter. Tell him how to succeed and how to keep his dream alive. (Write each sentence after the one before it to form a paragraph.)

Dear Oskar,

I know you have a dream. I know you want to succeed. You can do that, but you need to make some changes. _____

_____

_____

_____

_____

_____

_____

D Journal Assignment

Each day think about what you have to do or need to do. Write sentences in your journal about that. Next think of what you like doing. Write sentences about that.

Read from your journal to a classmate in class. Talk about what you wrote.

UNIT FOUR
CHAPTER 7
Work

A Prewriting

Exercise 1. Read, practice, and match Read these short conversations. Then practice them with your teacher. Next practice each one with a classmate.

1. I have a part-time job.
   A what?
   A part-time job.

2. The job begins at 7:00 A.M. and ends at 11:00 A.M.
   When?
   It begins at 7 and ends at 11.

3. The job is in the school library.
   Where is it?
   In the school library.

4. I need a job to earn money.
   Why?
   To earn money.

5. I work with a classmate.
   With who(m)?
   With a classmate.

6. I like my boss.
   Who(m) do you like?
   My boss.

7. My teacher comes to visit me.
   Who visits you?
   My teacher.

8. I go home by bus.
   How?
   By bus.

Read the dialogues again to help you match the question words to the answers.

A

1. ____ Who?
2. ____ Who(m)?
3. ____ When?
4. ____ Where?
5. ____ What?
6. ____ With who(m)?
7. ____ Why?
8. ____ How?

B

a. my teacher
b. to earn money
c. a part-time job
d. a classmate
e. in the school library
f. 7 to 11
g. my boss
h. by bus

Exercise 2. Create a story Look at the picture story. Use the words below to write two sentences for each picture. Some sentences use past tense. Some use present tense. You decide.

1.

   A. Abdullah / look for / job / school employment office

   B. Many other students / search for / jobs / too

   A. _____

   B. _____

2.

   A. Abdullah / work / checkout desk

   B. He like / work / there

   A. _____

   B. _____

3.

A. Abdullah / talk / his coworker
B. His coworker / be / classmate

A. _____
B. _____

4.

A. Abdullah / say / ?
B. His teacher / say / ?

A. _____
B. _____

What did Abdullah say to his teacher? What did the teacher say to Abdullah? Make up your own short conversation.

Exercise 3. Exchanging stories Write your sentences from Exercise 2 on a separate piece of paper. Begin with the first sentence. Continue with the next one to form a paragraph.

Pass your story to the person on your right. Read the story from the person to your left. When you are finished, talk about your stories with the group. Choose one story from your group to read to the class.

Exercise 4. Filling out a questionnaire A questionnaire has lots of questions. It is usually about a certain subject. This one is about *you*. Fill it out. This means write the answers to the questions.

Questions	Answers
What is your name?	
Where do you go to school?	
Who is your instructor?	
When do you come to school?	
How long do you study each day?	
Whom do you work with?	
Why do you work?	
Where do you work?	
How many hours a week do you study?	

B Structure

Exercise 1. Information questions Questions with the words **who, what, when, where, why,** and **how** are often called information questions. They ask for specific information.

Using Exercise 1 and Exercise 4 from the Prewriting section on this page and on page 60, make questions about Abdullah. The words that follow give information about Abdullah and are the answers to the questions you will write.

August 3rd	three brothers and two sisters	downtown
in the school library	to earn money for books	Abdullah Ben Sur
with my classmates	my English teacher	nineteen hours a week

EXAMPLE: September 6th
When does school start?

1. _____
2. _____
3. _____
4. _____
5. _____
6. _____
7. _____
8. _____
9. _____

Exercise 2. Facts about you   Think about yourself. Write down words and phrases that are facts about you and your life. Write down at least six facts on a separate piece of paper. You do not need to write complete sentences. Write your name on that paper.

> **EXAMPLE:** just one sister

Collect all the papers. Put them next to each other. Go around the group. Each person asks a question. The answer to the question is on one of the papers.

Exercise 3. Where do you come from? How do you get there?   "Where are you from?" and "Where do you come from?" are two questions with the same answer.

> **EXAMPLE:** Lou, where do you come from?   New York.
>
> Lou, where are you from?   New York.

"How do you get there?" is a question about direction and transportation. You give the direction and measure the distance or time from here, the place where you are right now.

> **EXAMPLE:** Lou, where do you come from?   New York.
>
> How do you get there?   You take a plane going
> (We are in Austin, Texas)   northeast.
>   (It takes about three hours.)

Stand up and move around. Ask each other the questions. Write down your classmates' answers on a piece of paper.

Unit 4: Work

 **Exercise 4. Class travel chart**   Follow your instructor's directions. You will build the class travel chart together.

Sentences about my classmates:

_____   _____
_____   _____
_____   _____
_____   _____
_____   _____
_____   _____
_____   _____
_____   _____
_____   _____
_____   _____

C Writing and Editing

Exercise 1. Abdullah's conversations   Abdullah talks to a lot of people in the library. Sometimes he mixes up words. Can you help him? Put the correct word in the blank.

EXAMPLE: Abdullah: "What do you come from?"

Student: "What did you say?"

Abdullah: "___*Where*___ do you come from?"

Chapter 7

1. Abdullah: "What do you live?"

   Student: "What did you say?"

   Abdullah: "_____ do you live?"

2. Abdullah: "How do you start work?"

   Student: "What was that?"

   Abdullah: "_____ do you start work?"

3. Abdullah: "When are you today?"

   Student: "What was that?"

   Abdullah: "_____ are you today?"

4. Abdullah: "Why is our final? 9 o'clock?"

   Student: "Come again?"

   Abdullah: "_____ is our final? 9 o'clock?"

5. Abdullah: "What much did you pay for that computer?"

   Student: "Excuse me?"

   Abdullah: "_____ much did you pay for that computer?"

6. Abdullah: "What is that girl crying?"

   Student: "Huh?"

   Abdullah: "_____ is that girl crying?"

7. Abdullah: "When gave you that watch?"

   Student: "Huh?"

   Abdullah: "_____ gave you that watch?"

Exercise 2. Abdullah's bad day Yesterday Abdullah had a bad day in the library. Help him tell his story. Write the correct form of the verb in the blank. If necessary, use Appendix III in the back of the book to help you with the irregular verbs.

Abdullah's Story

I _____ (like) my job, but yesterday I _____ (have) a bad day. Why? Because, first of all, I _____ (break) my clock radio alarm. I _____ (knock) it to the floor in the middle of the night. So I _____ (get up) late. I _____ (be) late for work in the library. Then my boss, Al, _____ (begin) to cough and sneeze. I _____ (try) to avoid talking to him. I _____ (do) not want to get sick. Next, I _____ (pick up) a heavy stack of books. I _____ (hurt) my back. It _____ (hurt) so bad, I _____ (have) to go home early. When I _____ (get) home, I _____ (start) to sneeze and cough.

Exercise 3. A bad day at work Think of the last time you had a bad day at work. What happened? Answer these questions with short answers.

1. When was it?

   _____

2. What job was it?

   _____

3. Where was your workplace?

   _____

4. What went wrong?

   _____

5. How did you feel?

   _____

6. What happened in the end?

   _____

Now write the story of your bad day. Write each sentence after the other to form a paragraph. Use the answers to the questions to tell the story.

_____
_____
_____
_____
_____
_____
_____
_____

Exercise 4. Reading and asking questions   Work with a classmate. Exchange stories. Read your classmate's story. Then write five questions about the story. Give the story back. Give your classmate the questions. Talk together about the stories and the answers to the questions.

D Journal Assignment

Think of a job you had, a job you have now, a job you would like to have. Write down all the words you can think of that go with that job. Practice speaking about the job for two minutes without stopping. Prepare to give a two-minute talk to your class about the job.

UNIT FOUR
CHAPTER 8
Work

A Prewriting

Exercise 1. Finding the story Look at the pictures on page 71 and read the sentences below. There are three sentences for each picture; two sentences describe the picture, and one does not. Copy the sentences that tell the story beside each picture.

1. These women are in the maternity ward of the hospital.

   The nurse is pushing the new mother in the wheelchair.

   The new mother is crying.

2. The mother is changing the baby's diaper.

   The baby is drinking a bottle.

   The mother is tired but happy.

3. The baby's father works in a factory.

   The baby's father works in an office in a hospital.

   His job is very stressful.

4. The mother teaches mathematics.

   The father is taking care of his son.

   The baby is laughing.

1.

2.

3.

4.

Exercise 2. Creating characters Fill in the chart that follows. Create an identity for some of the people in the pictures.

Name	Job	Pay	Problem	Satisfaction

Now use the chart to talk about the people in the picture story. Tell each other your stories.

Exercise 3. Defining tools A tool is something you use to do a job. A computer can be a tool. A hammer can be a tool. A frying pan can be a tool. They are tools if they are used to do a job.

Make a list of tools for each person in Exercise 2. Then think about what each person does with the tools.

Unit 4: Work

Now write five sentences about one person in the picture and five tools he or she uses.

                           (tool)   (what I do with the tool)
EXAMPLE: She uses a textbook to teach.

1. _____
2. _____
3. _____
4. _____
5. _____

Exercise 4. The day   Choose either the husband or the wife in the picture story on page 71. Imagine what his or her day is like. Complete the following schedule.

Person _____

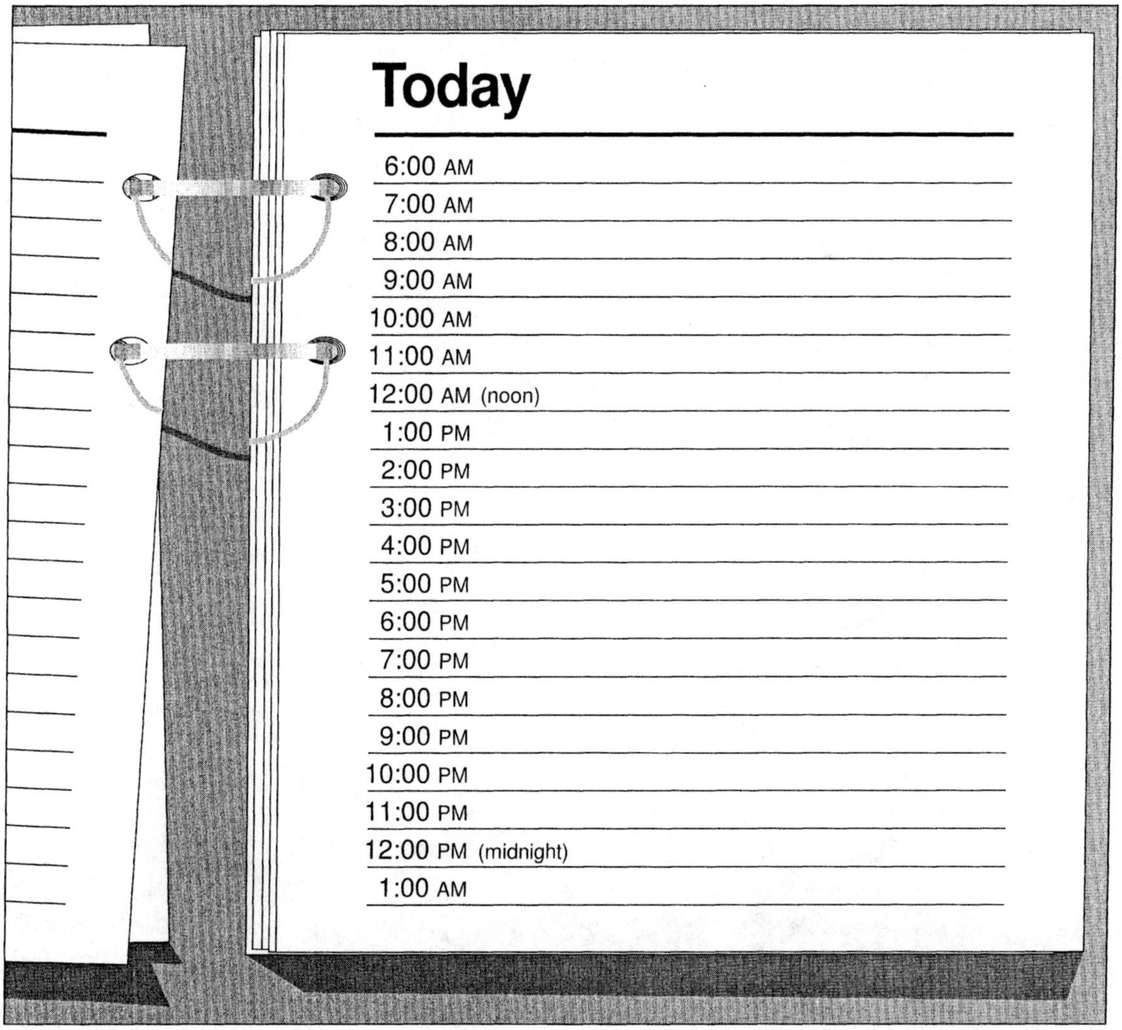

Today

6:00 AM	
7:00 AM	
8:00 AM	
9:00 AM	
10:00 AM	
11:00 AM	
12:00 AM (noon)	
1:00 PM	
2:00 PM	
3:00 PM	
4:00 PM	
5:00 PM	
6:00 PM	
7:00 PM	
8:00 PM	
9:00 PM	
10:00 PM	
11:00 PM	
12:00 PM (midnight)	
1:00 AM	

Chapter 8

Now, take turns talking about the schedule of the husband or the wife.

EXAMPLE: The wife wakes up at 6:00 in the morning.

The husband works at the hospital from 8:00 A.M. to noon.

B Structure

Exercise 1. Revisiting the story Go back to the sentences that you wrote under each picture on page 71. Rewrite the sentences below. Use pronouns wherever you can.

EXAMPLE: The nurse is examining a young woman.

She is examining **her.**

1. _____
2. _____
3. _____
4. _____
5. _____
6. _____
7. _____
8. _____

Exercise 2. Using pronouns First identify the italicized word or words as a subject **(S)** or object **(O)** noun. Then fill in the blank with the appropriate subject or object pronoun.

Pronouns

In English, pronouns are used after you know the noun.

Subject Pronouns		**Object Pronouns**	
I	we	me	us
you	you	you	you
he/she/it	they	him/her/it	them

EXAMPLE:

noun
The **nurse** is walking into the room. **She** is pushing a wheelchair.

EXAMPLE:

noun
The nurse examined the woman's **arm** and then bandaged **it.**

Unit 4: Work

1. *Bill* is a doctor. _____ works in a hospital.

2. *Bobby and Lisa* are sick. _____ are in bed.

3. *Andrea* takes good care of patients. _____ works in a hospital.

4. *The hospital* is an important building in a community. _____ is located in the center of town.

5. *My sister and I* waited in the emergency room. _____ were nervous.

6. *You and your friend* both want to be nurses. _____ have good plans.

7. *The children* all have colds. _____ can't go swimming.

8. *Dr. Maria Sanchez* performed the operation. _____ is a successful surgeon.

9. Twenty medical students were watching *Dr. Sanchez.* They learned from _____.

10. The doctor told *Sheila Brown* to change her diet. She told _____ to stop eating so many calories.

11. The doctor tells *all her patients* to watch what they eat. She tells _____ to eat more fruits and vegetables.

12. Dr. Sanchez is related to *my brother and me.* She visits _____ every Thanksgiving.

Exercise 3. A conversation Here is a conversation between a husband and wife about work. Write the correct pronoun for the italicized nouns.

EXAMPLE: Allan: Did you get your *paycheck?*

Sara: Yes, I got ___it___.

Allan
(the husband): Was *William* at the meeting?

Sara
(the wife): No, _____ wasn't there.

Allan: How about *Mr. Lee?*

Sara: Sure, _____ was there. _____'s the boss.

Chapter 8

Allan: Oh! Of course! *His wife* owns the company.

Sara: That's right. _____ does.

Allan: I bet *Mr. Lee and his wife* make a good team.

Sara: Yes, _____ do. You should know. You met _____ at our party.

Allan: Funny. I don't remember *that party* well.

Sara: I'm not surprised you don't remember _____. You had too much to drink. My brother had to drive you home. Don't you remember that?

Allan: You know, you and I should invite *the Lees* over for dinner.

Sara: Yes, let's invite _____ for next Friday.

 **Exercise 4. A poem to remember**   Read this poem aloud. Try to memorize it.

Him? Her?

Have you met him? Have you met her?

He likes you, you know.

Do you like him? Do you like her?

They talk about you—all the time.

Like me? Know me?

I don't know them.

Do you? Did we ever meet?

You and I? Did we meet them?

She knows us. He knows us.

I talk about you to them—all the time.

They like you already, already.

And you've never met.

C Writing and Editing

Exercise 1. Editing for pronouns Read the story below. There are mistakes in the italicized pronouns. Cross out the mistakes. Write in the correct pronouns.

Boomer's Story

Boomer Jones grew up near the railroad line. *Him* rode on trains all over the country. *She* loved to ride *they*. When he grew to a man, Boomer took a job on a passenger train. *She* loved *its*. But his real desire was to drive the train. *She* wanted to be a conductor. The owners of the railroad liked Boomer. But *them* didn't let *he* be a conductor. *Them* said *him* was not educated enough. To be a conductor, you needed a high school diploma. *They* didn't have one. So Boomer spent his life riding trains, but *she* could never drive *they*.

Now compare your stories.

Exercise 2. Editing for time order Read the sentences that follow. They are about Ivan Jacov. Ivan is a nurse. He works the night shift at Good Care Hospital. This story is about his work last night.

The story is not in the correct order of events. Change the numbers of each sentence to show the correct time order.

_____ 1. Ivan finished his shift at 8 A.M.

_____ 2. Ivan started his night duty in the emergency room.

_____ 3. He sat down for a cup of coffee at 3 A.M. after the operation.

_____ 4. At 1:00, he helped Dr. Sanchez in the operating room.

_____ 5. Around 12:30, a patient came in bleeding from a gunshot wound.

_____ 6. The patient needed emergency surgery.

_____ 7. Ivan made the rounds with Dr. Mills at 4 A.M.

_____ 8. From 5 A.M. until daylight, things were quiet at the hospital.

Chapter 8

_____ 9. Dr. Sanchez asked Ivan to get the patient ready for surgery.

_____ 10. Ivan came to her. She complained of chest pains.

_____ 11. At 4:30, Mrs. O'Dowd called out for a nurse.

_____ 12. Ivan called Dr. Mills to see Mrs. O'Dowd.

Now work by yourself and rewrite the story. Write one sentence after the other to form a paragraph.

Ivan's Night

Exercise 3. Questions about work You are going to write about your work. If you don't work, talk about the work of someone in your family. First, you need to organize your information. Let your partner ask you these questions. Write down notes about your answers.

EXAMPLE: Where do you work?
In a factory

1. Where do you work?

   _____

2. What hours do you work?

   _____

3. Who(m) do you work with?

   _____

Unit 4: Work

4. What is your position?

    _____

5. What are your responsibilities?

    _____

6. When do you feel good about your work?

    _____

7. When do you feel bad about your work?

    _____

8. What do you want to do next at your job? Do you want another position there? Do you want to change jobs?

    _____

9. How does this job help you now?

    _____

10. Do you expect to work at this job in the future?

    _____

Exercise 4. Writing about your work Use the information from Exercise 3, and write a story about your work or about the work of someone in your family.

_____

_____

_____

_____

_____

D Journal Assignment

In your journal, make a list of all the jobs that your family and friends have. Then choose one of the jobs to write about. Choose one you like. Write a short description of why you like the job.

Chapter 8

UNIT FIVE
CHAPTER 9

Leisure and Recreation

A Prewriting

Exercise 1. Vocabulary building These pictures are about a family. Ludo, Elena, and Sylvie work hard, but they also enjoy their free time. On page 81, write down what you see each person doing in the picture.

1.

2.

3.

4.

UNIT FIVE
CHAPTER 9

Ludo (the father)	**Elena** (the mother)	**Sylvie** (the daughter)

Tell each other what Ludo, Elena, and Sylvie are doing. Then tell your partner if you do it, too.

EXAMPLE: Sylvie is jogging. I jog, too.

The women in picture 2 are wearing slacks.

Exercise 2. Talking about hobbies A hobby is something you enjoy doing in your free time. It is different from a sport or from exercise. A hobby usually does not involve strong physical activity.

EXAMPLES: chess, gardening, stamp collecting, listening to music

Think of some more hobbies. Write them in the "Hobby" column.

Hobby	**Person**
_____	_____
_____	_____
_____	_____
_____	_____
_____	_____
_____	_____

Chapter 9

81

Now go around the classroom. Ask your classmates if they practice the hobbies on your list. Ask them, for example, "Do you play chess?" "Do you like gardening?" "Do you collect stamps?" When you find someone who answers yes, have that person sign his or her name in the column next to the hobby.

Exercise 3. Sports and exercise   In the first picture, Ludo is practicing tai chi. Tai chi is a gentle form of exercise. In the third picture, Sylvie is running cross country. Cross country running is a sport. Now think about yourself, your family, your friends, and your classmates. Then write four or five sentences about exercise and sports.

> **EXAMPLE:** My brother Angel practices judo.

_____

_____

_____

_____

_____

One person reads a sentence. The others listen. If you hear the same sport or form of exercise, then read your sentence and add *too*.

> **EXAMPLE:** My brother Angel practices judo.
>
> My friend Joseph practices judo, too.

Exercise 4. Describing a picture

1. Look at the four pictures and together choose one to describe. Write down all of the words that you think when you see the picture.

_____

_____

_____

_____

_____

_____

Unit 5: Leisure and Recreation

2. Divide the group into two parts. Take turns telling a story for the picture. Use all of the words you just wrote.

3. Find someone from another group. Sit down together. Close your eyes. Ask your new partner to tell you about his or her picture. Open your eyes. Look at the picture. Can you identify the words you heard?

4. Now you tell your story. Your partner closes his or her eyes.

B Structure

Exercise 1. Forming the continuous tense Use the present continuous tense **be + -ing** for actions that are happening "now." Fill in the missing parts for the following verbs.

Have
I _____ having   _____ are having
you _____ having   you are _____
he _____ having   they _____ having
she is _____
it _____ _____

Be
_____ am being   we _____ being
you are _____   you are _____
he _____ being   _____ are _____
she is _____
it _____ _____

Go
I _____ _____   _____ are _____
you _____ _____   _____ are _____
he _____ _____   _____ are _____
she _____ _____
it _____ _____

Exercise 2. What's happening? The present continuous tense focuses on things that are happening now. Use the words that follow to make sentences in the present continuous tense.

EXAMPLE: Ludo, practice, tai chi, in the park.
Ludo is practicing tai chi in the park.

1. Sylvie, run, cross country

   _____

2. Elena, read, poetry

   _____

3. Ludo, play, bass

   _____

4. Ludo, sip, coffee

   _____

5. Elena, listen to, Ludo

   _____

6. Sylvie, do, jigsaw puzzle

   _____

7. A fire, burn, in the fireplace

   _____

8. Two people, walking, their dog

   _____

9. Some guys, play, soccer

   _____

10. The girls, race, each other

    _____

Exercise 3. Pronouns and adjectives Add the correct possessive adjectives in the story that follows.

Here are the subject pronouns with their corresponding possessive adjectives.

Subject pronouns	Possessive pronouns
I own a car.	It's **my** car.
You own a guitar.	It's **your** guitar.
He owns a house.	It's **his** house.
She owns a necklace.	It's **her** necklace.
The pearls in **it** are real.	**Its** pearls are real.
We have three children.	We love **our** children.
You have five cats.	You love **your** cats.
They have three aunts.	They love **their** aunts.

Relaxing at Home

The Petrovs love to spend their free time at home. They love to be together in _____ living room. Ludo practices _____ bass. Elena and Sylvie do _____ jigsaw puzzle. Ludo makes a fire. Sylvie likes making popcorn. She serves it to _____ parents. They always enjoy _____ taste. Elena says to Ludo, "_____ bass playing sounds really good these days."

"Thanks, honey," he says, "Maybe it's because I love _____ audience."

"I hope so, Ludo. We should count _____ blessings. We are lucky to have this time together."

Chapter 9

Exercise 4. Relaxing Think about your free time at home. Think about the other people who live with you. Imagine that right now it is eight o'clock at night. Everyone is home. Everyone is relaxing. Where are they? What are they doing? What are you doing? Where are you? Write about it in the space provided. Write five pairs of sentences.

EXAMPLE: My brother is home. He's playing his guitar.

_____

_____

_____

_____

_____

Exchange books with your partner. Read silently. Underline the possessive adjectives (my, your, his, her, its, our, their) and the present continuous tense. Then ask your partner any questions you want to about his or her sentences.

EXAMPLE: <u>My</u> brother is home. He<u>'s playing</u> <u>his</u> guitar.
What kind of music can he play?

Exercise 5. Using *not* with the continuous tense In the first picture, Ludo is practicing tai chi. He is *not* jogging. We could also say or write: He **isn't** jogging. The **isn't** form is a contraction.

Full form	Contracted form
I am not jogging.	I'm not jogging.
You are not jogging.	You're not jogging.
He/She is not jogging.	He/She isn't jogging.
We are not jogging.	We aren't jogging.
You are not jogging.	You aren't jogging.
They are not jogging.	They aren't jogging.

Each sentence below tells what a person is doing. Write another sentence to tell what the person **isn't** doing.

    EXAMPLE: Ludo is practicing tai chi.
                                He isn't dancing.

1. Two people are walking their dog.

   _____

2. The guys are playing soccer.

   _____

3. The young mother is jogging with her baby.

   _____

4. Elena is reading poetry.

   _____

5. Ludo is sipping coffee.

   _____

6. Sylvie is running in a race.

   _____

7. Elena and Sylvie are doing a jigsaw puzzle.

   _____

8. Ludo is playing his bass.

   _____

9. I am working at the computer.

   _____

10. You are learning Spanish.

    _____

Chapter 9

C Writing and Editing

Exercise 1. Describing a scene When we describe what we see, we begin from one place or one person. We move to the next place or person. We create an order. This order helps the reader understand our writing. Read the sentences that follow. Then organize them by rewriting them in order.

1. Ludo is sitting with Sylvie.
2. Ludo and Sylvie are drinking coffee.
3. Elena is on stage.
4. Elena is reading poetry.
5. The coffeehouse is full of people.
6. Some people are talking to each other.
7. Some people are listening to the poets.
8. Ludo and Sylvie are listening to Elena.

Now rewrite the sentences in order. Write one sentence after another to form a paragraph.

_____
_____
_____
_____
_____
_____

Exercise 2. Editing the story Go back to Exercise 1. Find where there are two sentences together about the same person or people. In the second sentence, cross out the name of the person or the names of the people. Write in a pronoun instead.

EXAMPLE: Sylvie is doing the puzzle. ~~Sylvie~~ *She* is doing the puzzle with Elena.

Exercise 3. Imagining yourself a star   Close your eyes and imagine. Think of a hobby or sport that you are doing. See yourself doing that hobby or sport. Everything is fine. You are doing it very well. There are other people there, too. Everyone knows that you are doing very well. Look around. What do you see? Where are you? What time of day is it? Who are the other people? What are you doing?

Open your eyes. Now write sentences about that scene.

_____

_____

_____

_____

_____

_____

_____

Exercise 4. Editing for details   Read your sentences to your group. After everyone reads, think about who has the most details.

Go back to Exercise 3 and add one or two more details to make your writing clearer.

D Journal Assignment

Get a newspaper. Find the sports section or the lifestyle section. Find a picture, cut it, and paste it in your journal. Write about your picture. What is it about? What do you think about it?

UNIT FIVE
CHAPTER 10

Leisure and Recreation

A Prewriting

1.
2.
3.
4.

Exercise 1. Matching sentences with pictures Read the sentences that follow. Decide which picture on page 90 they go with. Then rewrite each one beside its picture.

a. They're watching a music video.
b. They're walking and enjoying the performers.
c. They're having a tea party.
d. They're discussing a piece of furniture.
e. They aren't watching a movie.
f. They aren't shopping for a television.
g. They aren't dancing in the street.
h. They aren't playing soccer at school.
i. It's probably raining outside.
j. It's a beautiful summer day.
k. It's probably a little cold outside.
l. It's a spring morning.

Exercise 2. Free time activities Here is the English alphabet. For each letter, write the name of a hobby or free time activity. Write on a large piece of paper. Some letters may be very difficult. Here are some examples.

A - going to **art** shows
B -
C -
D -
E -
F -
G -
H -
I -
J - bungee **jumping**
K -
L -
M -
N -
O -
P -
Q - (difficult)
R -
S -
T -
U -
V -
W -
X - (difficult)
Y -
Z - going to the **zoo**

Put the papers with the lists on the wall of the classroom. Walk around and read the other lists. Do you know all these activities? If you don't, ask someone.

EXAMPLE: Student 1: "**Bee keeping?** What is bee keeping?"
Student 2: "It's when you have bees. You take care of them. You get honey."

Exercise 3. The television guide Below is a morning television guide. Read each program and description. Guess what kind of program each one is. Tell each other if you watch programs like these.

MORNING

(CC) Program is closed-captioned for the hearing impaired

	2:00 AM to 6:00 AM	6:00 AM	6:30 AM	7:00 AM	7:30 AM	8:00 AM	8:30 AM
WRAP Channel **77**	Off air	**Morning Yoga with Lola** Lola teaches the lotus position.	**Early Morning National News** Joe O'Hare and Kuki Chang (CC) **(6:50) Local News Summary** Ramon Wang (CC)	**Good Day People** Muffy welcomes artist Cosmo Dome, singing group The New Plastic Boys, Chef Zito cooks home fries			
	9:00 AM	9:30 AM	10:00 AM	10:30 AM	11:00 AM	11:30 AM	12:00 AM (noon)
	Irma Live! When good things happen to bad people, interviews with millionaires who got their money by cheating other people			**Animal Court** Veterinarian and Judge Honest Days rules on stolen parrot, barking dogs, and poisoned goldfish.		**The World Never Turns** Agnes discovers Betty is her sister, Betty finds out her new boyfriend is her father, Abe; Abe has a midlife crisis	**Happy News at Noon** Joe and Kuki join Ramon for local and national news and entertainment gossip (CC)

Exercise 4. At the movies Here are some kinds of movies. Tell each other which kinds of movies you have seen. Tell each other about the stars of the movies. Talk about the plot (the story). Use the chart that follows to help you.

western   musical   science fiction   historical drama
adventure   comedy   drama   mystery/crime

Movies I Have Seen			
Name of Movie	Type of Movie	Stars	Rating: ♦ = bad ♦♦♦♦ = great

Unit 5: Leisure and Recreation

B Structure

Exercise 1. Using demonstrative adjectives, *this* and *that* Read each pair of sentences. Rewrite the sentences into one sentence with **this** or **that**.

EXAMPLE: The book is in front of me. It is my writing book.
This is my writing book.

> ### This and That
>
> Use **this** to point out things that are near you. Use **that** to point out things that are not so near to you.
>
> **EXAMPLES:** I am writing on a computer in my study. The computer is right in front of me.
> I say: **This** computer is fast and powerful.
>
> There is another computer in my house. It is not in this room. It is not in front of me.
> I say: **That** computer is slow and not powerful.

1. The car is in front of me. It is new.

2. The house is down the street. It is yellow and white.

3. The rose is in my hand. It smells good.

4. The table is across the room. It is white.

5. The movie is playing in a theater downtown. It is a western.

6. The tennis racket is in my shoulder bag. It is broken.

Chapter 10

Exercise 2. Demonstrative adjectives, *these* and *those* Change these sentences using **these** or **those**.

> ### *These* and *Those*
>
> **These** and **those** are the plural forms of **this** and **that**. Notice that the prepositional phrases of location, for example *in this lab,* are not necessary when you use the demonstrative adjectives.
>
> **EXAMPLES:** The computers in this lab are Macs.
> **These** computers are Macs.
>
> The computers in the lab across campus are PCs.
> **Those** computers are PCs.

1. The windows in this room are big.

   _____

2. The desks in that classroom are small.

   _____

3. The instructors in this department are fun.

   _____

4. The actors in that movie were terrible.

   _____

5. The comedian at that club isn't funny.

   _____

6. The game we are playing is lots of fun.

   _____

Exercise 3. *This, that, these,* and *those*. What have you got? Work with a classmate. Face each other. Take objects out of your pockets and your book bag. Make sure they are the same objects. Put the objects in front of both of you. Put one near you. Put the other near your partner. Now point to an object. Say something about it.

> **EXAMPLE:** (Point to notebook)
> That notebook has a black cover. It's my notebook.

Then, take the notebook or give it to your partner. Continue until there is nothing left.

Exercise 4. Another look at the pictures Look at the pictures at the beginning of the chapter. Take turns talking about the pictures. Use **this, that, these,** and **those** as much as you can.

> **EXAMPLE:** Picture 1. **These** girls are very interested in the TV program.

When you have finished talking, choose pictures 1 and 2 or 3 and 4. Write sentences about the pictures. Write eight sentences using **this, that, these,** and **those.**

1. _____
2. _____
3. _____
4. _____
5. _____
6. _____
7. _____
8. _____

C Writing and Editing

Exercise 1. Editing the story Jill is shopping for a new car. Look at the pictures that follow. Fill in the blank spaces with **this, that, these,** or **those**.

I can't decide which car to buy!

_____ one is very practical, but _____ one is so beautiful!

_____ one is very expensive, but _____ one is boring.

A. What is your opinion? Which car should Jill buy? _____

Charlie is shopping for new shoes.

I can't decide which shoes to buy!

_____ shoes are very expensive, but _____ shoes are ugly.

_____ shoes are not so expensive, but _____ shoes are so cool!

B. What is your opinion? Which shoes should Charlie buy? _____

 Now make a similar story for your partner to read. Exchange stories. Then read your partner's story and write the answers.

Exercise 2. Putting the story in order Read the sentences. Then rewrite them into a story. Write one sentence after the other to form a paragraph.

1. Sven thinks that it is Japanese, but Kip thinks it's a Korean rice chest.

2. A few minutes ago, Sven and Kip stopped in front of an antique shop.

3. Now, Kip and Sven are discussing one of the chests.

Unit 5: Leisure and Recreation

4. The shop will deliver it next week.

5. Finally, they decide to buy it.

6. The shopkeeper says that Kip is right. It is Korean.

7. They stopped because they both were attracted by the oriental chests and pottery.

Exercise 3. Imagine yourself Imagine yourself walking down a city street. It is Sunday afternoon. It is springtime. The sun is shining. Trees and flowers are blooming. You are walking in a shopping area. There are a lot of restaurants and cafes. You walk around, looking at the people and the shops. One shop catches your eye. You stop to look in the window. You see something you like, and you go into the shop. You ask to see that thing. You ask how much it is. You always wanted something like this. You know it will make you happy. You buy it. You take it home.

Write the story in the space provided. Write about what you bought.

Exercise 4. Giving feedback on your partner's story Exchange stories with a partner. Read your partner's story and answer the questions in the following chart. Use the chart to edit your partner's story.

What my partner bought . . .

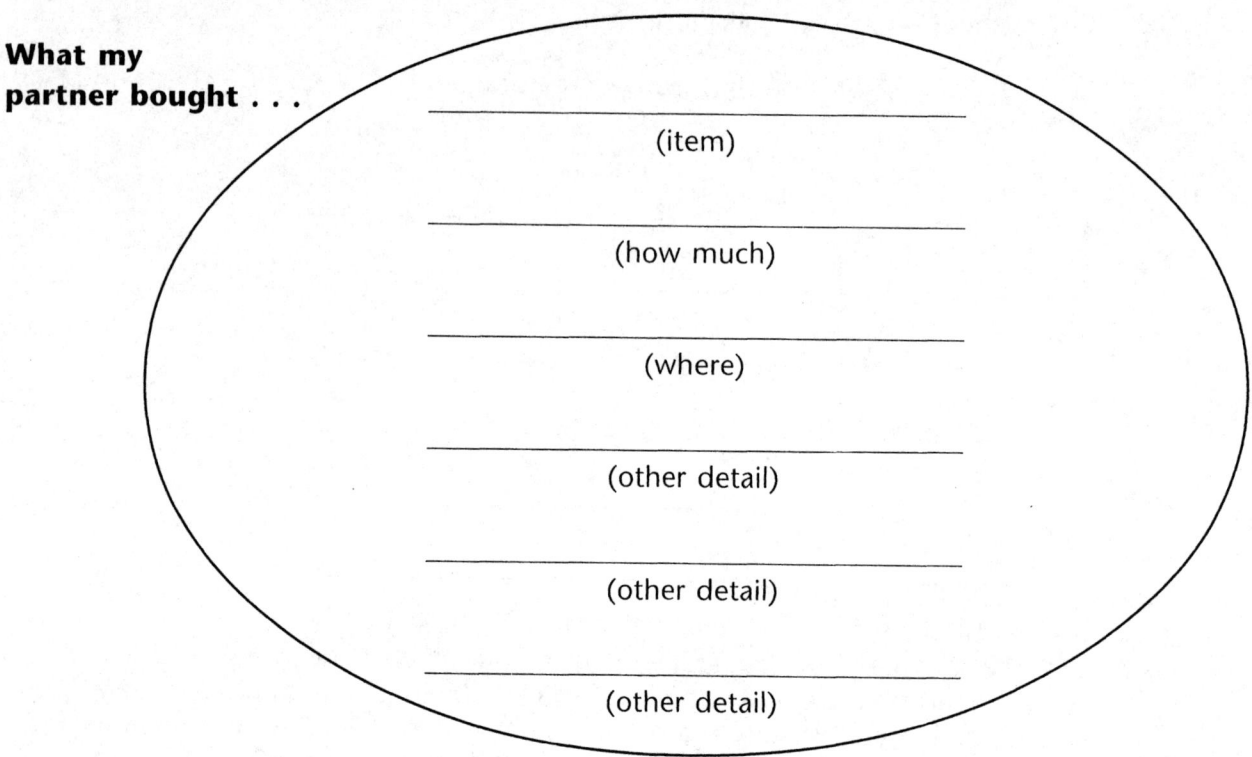

(item)

(how much)

(where)

(other detail)

(other detail)

(other detail)

Now write two questions to get more information you want to know about your partner's story.

1. _____

2. _____

Now read the feedback from your partner. Answer the questions. Add more details, and then rewrite your story on a sheet of paper.

D Journal Assignment

Think about five shops or stores that you go to a lot. What kind of shop or store is it? What do you buy there? Who works there? What do they do? How do you pay for your purchases? Write about each of the five in your journal.

The Natural World

UNIT SIX
CHAPTER 11

A Prewriting

Exercise 1. Labeling the pictures Each person in the group works with one of the pictures. Write on or near the picture. Write the name of everything you see in the picture. Then share your words with the group.

1.

2.

3.

4.

Exercise 2. Making categories Work with the words from the pictures. Put them into two lists. One list is for natural things. The other list is for human-made things.

Natural things	Human-made things
_____	_____
_____	_____
_____	_____
_____	_____
_____	_____
_____	_____
_____	_____
_____	_____
_____	_____

Exercise 3. What happened? Each person talks about two pictures. Be sure to discuss the changes from one picture to the next. Then write the changes in the space provided.

EXAMPLE: There were a lot of trees. Now there aren't many trees.

Changes from picture 1 to picture 2

_____

_____

_____

_____

_____

Changes from picture 2 to picture 3

_____

_____

_____

_____

Changes from picture 3 to picture 4

_____

_____

_____

_____

Exercise 4. Changes in your hometown Think about your hometown. What changes have taken place over the years? List them in the space provided.

	Before	**Now**
EXAMPLE:	There were many homes across the street.	Now there is a bridge there.

Before   **Now**

_____   _____

_____   _____

_____   _____

_____   _____

_____   _____

Exchange lists with your partner. Read silently. Then ask each other questions.

EXAMPLE: Did your friends live in those houses? How do you feel about the bridge? Do you like it?

B Structure

Exercise 1. What has happened? One way to show that things have changed over time is to use the perfect tense. Here is an example of the present perfect tense with the verb *change*.

I have changed	we have changed
you have changed	you have changed
he/she/it has changed	they have changed

Notice that the present perfect tense uses the present tense of the verb **have** plus the **past participle** of the main verb. The past participle of regular verbs end in **-ed.** There are many irregular past participles. Some irregular past participles are listed in Appendix III. Now read the sentences below. Then write a sentence with the verb *change*.

    EXAMPLE: Bob is heavier now.
                    He has changed.

1. Donna is friendlier these days. _____

2. Bob and Donna don't smoke anymore. _____

3. I lost twenty pounds. _____

4. You don't say hello anymore. _____

5. The dog runs very slowly now. _____

6. Bob is very talkative now. _____

7. You and I study hard now. _____

Now match each sentence that follows with a preceding one.

_____ a. We didn't study hard before.

_____ b. They smoked a lot last year.

_____ c. I was very heavy six months ago.

_____ d. He was once a very quiet person.

_____ e. It ran very fast when it was a puppy.

_____ f. She was a cold person.

_____ g. You were very friendly.

Exercise 2. Another look at the pictures Look again at the picture story at the start of this chapter. Write ten sentences that show change. Use the perfect tense as much as possible.

   EXAMPLE: There were a lot of trees.
   Someone has cut down a lot of the trees.

1. _____
2. _____
3. _____
4. _____
5. _____
6. _____
7. _____
8. _____
9. _____
10. _____

Exercise 3. Things we still do You have hobbies, interests, skills, and habits that continue over time. Maybe you learned to ride a bicycle at age 5. Now you ride your bicycle in your free time. One way to say this is:

   EXAMPLE: I learned to ride a bike at age 5. I still ride in my free time.

   I **have ridden** a bike for a very long time.

Look at the following list of activities. Write about the ones that are true for *you*. Make sentences. Past participles are in parentheses.

tie (tied) my shoes	write (written) letters	bake (baked) bread
read (read) books	play (played) cards	play (played) chess
play (played) pool	speak (spoken) English	look (looked) at the stars
sew (sewn) clothes	knit (knitted) sweaters	see (seen) music concerts
fix (fixed) cars	go (gone) skiing	be (been) a student
practice (practiced) judo	collect (collected) CDs	program (programmed) computers

Add two more ideas of your own _____

_____

1. _____
2. _____
3. _____
4. _____
5. _____
6. _____
7. _____
8. _____
9. _____
10. _____

Exercise 4. Your classmates' experience   Write ten questions in the space provided using the topics in Exercise 3. In these questions, you are asking about your classmates' past experiences.

After you write your questions, go around the room and ask each person a question. If the person answers yes, write his or her name in the space next to the question. Try to get a different name for each question.

EXAMPLE: bake
Have you ever baked bread?

Questions   **Names**

1. _____   _____
2. _____   _____
3. _____   _____
4. _____   _____
5. _____   _____
6. _____   _____
7. _____   _____
8. _____   _____
9. _____   _____
10. _____   _____

C Writing and Editing

Exercise 1. Edit the conversation   Read the conversation between Nimita and David and correct the mistakes.

Nimita: "Has you ever gone to Sherwood Forest?"

David: "No, I haven't goed yet, but I want to. Is it far from here?"

Nimita: "About two hours away. Have you saw Bald Mountain?"

David: "Yes, I ever have."

Nimita: "It's beautiful. I has been there many times."

David: "I've only be there once. But I had a good time. I like hiking in the mountains."

Nimita: "Really? Have you ever climbing Mt. Whitney?"

David: "No. Has you?"

Nimita: "Yes, I have. I even climbed it last year."

David: "Wow! You're a real climber! I'm just a casual hiker."

Exercise 2. My favorite place   Think of your favorite place in nature. Maybe it's the mountains. Maybe it's the beach. Maybe it's the forest. Draw a picture of that place below.

Now answer these questions about that place.

1. When did you first go there?
   _____

2. How often do you go there?
   _____

3. Have you been there lately?
   _____

4. How do you get there?
   _____

5. What do you do there?
   _____

6. Do you go there alone or with others?
   _____

7. Has the place changed over time? How?
   _____

8. What do you like most about this place?
   _____

Now exchange books and read your classmate's questions and answers. Ask him or her more questions about the place. He or she will do the same for you. Take notes.

Exercise 3. Writing a story Write a story about your favorite place. Use the answers to the questions in Exercise 2 and any other information. Write one sentence after the other to form a paragraph.

My Favorite Place

___

Exercise 4. Reviewing capitalization and punctuation Read the story below. Pay attention to periods (.), commas (,), and capital letters. Make any changes necessary.

my FAVORITE Place

my favorite place is yosemite Park, it is near FRESNO, CALIFORNIA. The first time i went there was SIX YEARS ago . I go there once a year BUT I haven't been there for almost two years, I drive there from my home, It takes about five hours.. I mostly hike at yosemite, and I usually go with my FAMILY., Yosemite has gotten more crowded over the years but it is still very beautiful especially during spring snows, that's my favorite time.,.

Unit 6: The Natural World

 **Exercise 5. Nature's friend** Here is an unfinished poem. Put in your own words to complete it.

Nature's Friend

I am nature's friend

I have _____

Again and again.

I am nature's lover

I have _____

Over and over.

I am nature's child

I like _____

Wild, wild, wild.

I am nature's man (woman)

I have _____

Again and again.

 Read your poem to your group.

D Journal Assignment

In your daily life, notice nature around you. Write down what you see, what you hear, what you smell, what you touch, what you taste. Write down what you experience of nature every day.

UNIT SIX
CHAPTER 12

The Natural World

A Prewriting

Exercise 1. Where would you rather be?   Look at the four pictures. Don't worry about vocabulary words. Just look and get a feeling. Where would you rather be? In which picture? Why? Tell a classmate.

1.

2.

3.

4.

Exercise 2. What's there? Pick a picture and write down as many words as you know that are in the picture.

Now show the group your words. Together make a list of words for the four pictures. Write them in the following chart.

Picture 1	Picture 2	Picture 3	Picture 4

Exercise 3. More vocabulary Look at the words below. Decide which picture they belong with. Add them to the preceding chart.

humid   steamy   thick   strong   icy   barren

empty   dry   windy   rainy   calm   clear

ideal   awful   unbearable   dangerous   frightening

extreme   sunny   stormy

Chapter 12

Exercise 4. Wild places   Think about wild places. These places have few people, mostly nature. Sometimes the weather is very extreme. You need special clothing or equipment. You can only be there for a short time. Are there any wild places in your country? Write their names in the space provided.

1. _____
2. _____
3. _____
4. _____

Now choose one place to tell your classmates about. Write the words in the space provided that you will need to talk about that place.

_____
_____
_____
_____
_____

Each person speaks for one minute about a wild place. Another person keeps time. At the end of the speech, the group members ask the person questions.

B Structure

Exercise 1. Where would you rather go?   Your instructor will give you two choices. You choose one. Then pick a partner and talk to him or her for one minute. Begin by saying: *I'd rather . . . because . . .*

> **EXAMPLE:** Would you rather go to a shopping mall or to the beach?
> *I'd rather go to a shopping mall because I just love to shop.*

Choices

jungle	desert
movies	concert
library	computer lab
mountain	island
country	city
zoo	museum

Unit 6: The Natural World

Exercise 2. I've never, but I'd like to   Look at the list of places in Exercise 1. If you have not been to a place, you write the following:

EXAMPLE: *I have never been to India.*

If it is a place you think you might like, you can write the following:

EXAMPLE: *I've never been to India, but I'd like to go.*

Write as many sentences as you can.

_____

_____

_____

Exercise 3. What can you do there?   Look at each picture from the beginning of this chapter. Each picture shows a different place. There are things that you *can do* and things you *can't do* in each place. For each picture, write things you can and can't do. Follow the example. Fill in the chart that follows.

EXAMPLE: (Picture 1) You can climb there. You can't swim there.

	Picture 1	Picture 2	Picture 3
can do	climb		
can't do	swim		

Chapter 12

Exercise 4. Making choices Making choices means deciding between two or more things or activities. Take turns giving choices. Write down your partner's answer. The first five choices are given below.

EXAMPLE: We can swim or we can hike. Which would you rather do?
I'd rather swim.

1. go to the mountains, go to the beach
2. swim in a pool, swim in the ocean
3. camp in the desert, camp in the jungle
4. rent a car, rent bikes
5. leave today, leave tomorrow

Now use the chart in Exercise 3 to give more choices.

6. _____
7. _____
8. _____

C Writing and Editing

Exercise 1. Editing for tense Read the story. Correct the verb tenses if they are wrong.

A Wild Place

Last night I have a dream. I dreamed that I driving my car out to the desert. The day is sunny. But later the wind began to blow very hard. I was looking for desert roses. Desert roses were natural sand formations that looked like flowers. I thought they are very beautiful. I pull off the road and stopping the car. I get out. I start to walk into the desert. There is no road. I walk toward a large sand dune. The wind blow even harder. I cannot see. I am lost. I became frightened. Then I see a cave. I seen a light inside the cave. There is somebody inside the cave.

Unit 6: The Natural World

Exercise 2. Continuing the story Write an ending to the story in the space provided.

_____

_____

_____

Exercise 3. Writing about a wild place In Exercise 4 on page 112, you spoke about a wild place in your country. Now, write down what you said. Write one sentence after another to form a paragraph.

_____

_____

_____

_____

_____

_____

_____

_____

Exercise 4. Group editing project Exchange your stories about a wild place with another group of four students in your class. Next read one of the stories from the new group. Edit for spelling, capital letters, verb tenses, and vocabulary words. Make changes above the writing. Use a pencil. Pass the story to your group mate. Each person in the group reads each story from the other group. Each person makes corrections and suggestions. When you are finished, give the other group its papers back.

Read the corrections and changes. Rewrite your story about a wild place. Then put it up on the classroom wall so that everyone can read it.

D Journal Assignment

Find out about the nature around you. Ask people about wild places in your area. Write about one of them in your journal.

APPENDIX

Appendix 1
Basic Capitalization and Punctuation Rules

Capitalization

- Every sentence always begins with a capital letter.
    - EX.   This country is very big.

- The word *I* is always capitalized.
    - EX.   My classmate and **I** walk to class.

- People's names are always capitalized.
    - EX.   Today I worked with **E**lvia, **V**ladimir, and **A**ki.

- Languages (English, Russian), countries (Canada, Australia), and people from countries (Korean, French) are always capitalized.
    - EX.   Some **C**anadians speak **E**nglish as a first language and some people from **C**anada speak **F**rench.

- School subjects do not have capital letters.
    - EX.   arithmetic, biology, calculus, dance, economics

- Jobs in education do not have capital letters.
    - EX.   professor, teacher, instructor, classroom aide

- Job titles have capital letters.
    - EX.   Professor Smith, Director of Admissions, President Carter

- Names of languages have capital letters.
    - EX.   Albanian, Chinese, English

- Names of schools have capital letters.
    - EX.   Near East University, Happy College

- Academic degrees have capital letters.
    - EX.   A.A., B.S., M.B.A., Ph.D.

Punctuation

- Every sentence ends with a period (**.**), an exclamation point (**!**), or a question mark (**?**).
    - **EX.** I live in Texas**.** What a big state**!** Have you been to Texas**?**

- An apostrophe (**'**) shows possession. Use **'s** with a singular noun. Use **s'** with a plural noun.
    - **EX.** This is my cousin**'s** book. This is my cousin**s'** house.

- Periods are used in abbreviations (shortened forms of words).
    - **EX.** Education Dept.   (Department)
        - Prof. Sills   (Professor)
        - Dr. Nash   (Doctor)
        - Pres. Young   (President)

Appendix II
Spelling Rules for Verbs

Simple Present Tense—Third Person

- For most verbs, add **-s**
    - **EX.** He work**s**

- Verbs that end in **-y** change to **-ies**.
    - **EX.** She stud**ies**.
        - He tr**ies**.

- Verbs that end in a vowel followed by **-y** do not change to **ies**.
    - **EX.** He pla**ys**.
        - She sa**ys**.

Present Continuous Tense

- One syllable verbs that are made up of consonant + vowel + consonant double the final consonant.

get	getting
run	running

- One syllable verbs that end in consonant + **e** drop the **e**.

drive	driving
make	making

Simple Past Tense

- For most regular verbs, add **-ed**.

work	worked
talk	talked

- Words ending in consonant + **y** drop the **y** and add **-ied**.

study	studied
try	tried

- Words ending in vowel + **y** follow the rule for regular verbs.

play	played
enjoy	enjoyed

- For words that end with consonant(s) + vowel + consonant, double the final consonant and add **-ed**.

plan	planned
shop	shopped

Appendix

Appendix III
Verbs

Present and Past Tense of the Verb be

Present Tense
I am   we are
you are   you are
he, she, it is   they are

Past Tense
I was   we were
you were   you were
he, she, it was   they were

Irregular Past Tense and Past Participles for Common Verbs

Base Form	Irregular Past Form	Irregular Past Participles
be	was, were	been
become	became	become
begin	began	begun
break	broke	broken
bring	brought	brought
buy	bought	bought
come	came	come
do	did	done
eat	ate	eaten
find	found	found
forget	forgot	forgotten
get	got	gotten
give	gave	given
go	went	gone

(Continued)

Base Form	Irregular Past Form	Irregular Past Participles
grow	grew	grown
have	had	had
hear	heard	heard
hurt	hurt	hurt
keep	kept	kept
know	knew	known
leave	left	left
make	made	made
put	put	put
read	read	read
ride	rode	ridden
run	ran	run
say	said	said
see	saw	seen
sell	sold	sold
send	sent	sent
sit	sat	sat
speak	spoke	spoken
stand	stood	stood
take	took	taken
teach	taught	taught
think	thought	thought
understand	understood	understood
wear	wore	worn
write	wrote	written

Appendix

Common Verbs Followed by to (infinitive) or -ing (gerund)

Verbs Followed by Infinitive	Verbs Followed by Gerund
want	like, dislike
need	enjoy
have	finish
ask	discuss
plan	practice
learn	keep
decide	appreciate
agree	mind
expect	quit
refuse	regret

Appendix IV
Journal Writing

Journals are notebooks in which writers keep a record of ideas, opinions, and descriptions of daily life. Journals help writers develop their creativity. In writing classes, instructors often ask students to write in journals.

Each writing instructor has different ideas about journal writing. Your instructor will tell you how to keep your journal and will probably collect it at certain times during the semester. Your instructor may write reactions to what you write and offer suggestions for vocabulary or improving your grammar. The main point of keeping a journal as a language student is to give you a chance to write about your ideas without worrying about a grade or correct grammar and usage. Journal writing is practice in writing and thinking.

Buy a standard size notebook with lined paper. Make this notebook your journal for this writing class only. Write nothing else in it. Do not write other class assignments in your journal. There are many rewards from keeping a journal, in addition to the informal conversation that takes place in it between you and yourself, and you and your instructor: when you have finished the course, you will have a record of what you read, what you experienced, and what you thought about during that time.

At the end of each chapter in this book, you will find some topics related to the theme of the unit. Write about them in your journal.

Glossary of Grammatical Terms

base form   The base form is also called the simple form. It is the infinitive without *to*. Example: *go*

consonant   A letter that does not have a vowel sound. In English, there are 21 consonants.

demonstrative adjectives   *this, that, these, those*

negation   Changing the verb to negative. Examples: *She **isn't** here. I **don't** work. They're **not** going. They have**n't** been.*

object   The receiver of an action. It is a noun. Example: *He gave the book to his **sister.***

object pronouns   *me, you, him, her, it, us, them*

past participle   The verb form used in perfect tenses. Regular past participles end in **ed**. There are many irregular past participles (see Appendix III for a list of common irregular past participles).

plural   Plural nouns are more than one noun. Examples: *books, children, women*

possessive adjectives   *my, your, his, her, its, our, their*

preposition   There are many small words that show location, direction, and time. Examples: *to, in, at, on, from, over*

prepositional phrase   A prepositional phrase is a group of words beginning with a preposition. Examples: *in high school, to the store*

pronouns   Pronouns take the place of nouns. Example: ***My sister** is a singer. **She** is a singer.*

question word order   The normal word order for questions is (Question word) verb + subject or (Question word) auxiliary verb + subject + verb. Examples: *Where was he? Where did he go? Did he go?*

question words   *who(m), what, when, where, which, why, how, how long*

singular   Singular nouns are only one. Examples: *book, child, woman*

statement word order   Normal word order for statements is subject + verb (+ object). Example: *I love English.*

subject   Every sentence has a subject and verb. The subject tells who or what is doing or experiencing something. Example: *I come from China.*

subject pronouns   *I, you, he, she, it, we, they*

verb   Every sentence has a subject and verb. The verb tells what the subject is doing or experiencing. Example: *He **comes** from China.*

vowel   A letter with the sound of **a, e, i, o, u.**